Collage by Kerry Sullivan

GREEN BAY
LOVE STORIES
and
OTHER AFFAIRS

By
Sandy Sullivan

First published by AuthorHouse 07/28/04

ISBN: 1-4184-6341-8 (e-book)
ISBN: 1-4184-3415-9 (Paperback)
ISBN: 1-4184-3417-5 (Dust Jacket)

Library of Congress Control Number: 2004092128

Printed in the United States of America
Bloomington, IN

This book is printed on acid free paper.

Dedicated to…
all the women who do so much to make
their heroes great….

Dedicated to those I love…
in loving memory of my cousin,
Kelly Ann Moran-Ward,
who would delight in this book…

and especially dedicated to my daughter,
Kerry Kate.

About the book:

It is doubtful if another woman has so openly and boldly shared with us her personal and private experiences with a professional football team. In fact, few women have had the opportunity or ability to fit in with the "guys" and create friendships which have endured for a lifetime. Love, laughter, and tears mix in this riveting and slightly risqué love story, and the home-spun philosophy causes one to pause and consider the validity of the remarks. Both <u>women</u> and <u>men</u> find themselves captured by the frank and endearing stories of individuals who are household names to **Green Bay Fans**, and they enjoy tidbits of pro-football history, as well as interesting and relatively unknown facts interwoven throughout the text. It is a love affair, encompassing comedy and tragedy, which started and will end with a lifelong passion to be part of what goes on in **Lambeau Field**. Where does a woman fit into this picture? Modeled and tested by the **Champions of Green Bay**, this author expresses deep and honest feelings about the lessons learned from relationships with players which shaped and directed her life, and tells us what it was like for <u>her</u>… to run with the "PACK."

TABLE OF CONTENTS

Acknowledgements

Few people have kinder family and friends than me. That is why I want to thank those who gave me the support I needed to start and finish this project.

My thanks to Jack McManus and Wallene Feldman, who listened and read for many hours when I am sure they did not want to, and it is their endless encouragement which helped me to continue when I did not want to. Thanks to my daughter, Kerry, who gave me permission to tell my tale. Thanks to my aunt, Maxine Lawrence, whose sacrifices helped make it happen, and my aunt, Genevieve Moran, who always had time for me. Special thanks to my wonderful parents, Ollie and Harold Steiner, whose love instilled in me the need for faith, courage, honor, and the will to survive.

The others who helped are listed here. I hope i have not left anyone out. My apologies if I have, and regardless, I thank you: Bonnie Vaughan, Barbara Adler, Emmy Burns, Rita Campbell, Kelly Backenkeller, Katie/Joey Bivona, Alicia Mahr, Don McKenzie, O.J. Navis, Karen/Stacy Harer, Manny/Ellie Harn, Sarajayne Griffin, Paul Hornung, Donny Anderson, Susan Ann/Fred Thurston, Jerry Kramer, Willie Wood, Ron Kramer, Dan Currie, Doug Moe, Max McGee, Mary Jane Sorgel, Alicia Huber, Suzanna/Bjorn Sjogren, Chris/Mimi Sullivan, Colleen/Ray Firenze, Kelly Reigel, Menzi Behrnd-Klodt, Ernestine/Henry Wagner, Jackie Brost, Jim Mayfield & Joe Tovano, for the awesome website, Domanic Scardino & Mark Kruesel, for marketing ideas, K.C. Chief fan, Clayton McGonigle, the Green Bay Packers, all of my other supportive friends, and wonderful students. Thanks to Henry A. Behrnd, former curator of the Elvehjem Museum, Madison WI who encouraged me to share these love stories with others. Thanks to Tom Miller for hiring me to work for the Green Bay Packers, so very long ago.

Thanks to my heavenly Father for his endless gifts, and for allowing me to remember what happened so long ago. I especially want to thank Him for the practice of trust, obedience, and perseverance which I have developed as a result of the lessons He has so generously given, and so patiently taught.

Heartfelt thanks to those who read my book. I hope you enjoy it, and will perhaps, learn from it…it was written for you.

Sandy Sullivan (2004)

FOREWARD

Dear Reader,

When we met in 1961, Sandy was 19 and I was 24 years old. Just kids!

The youth of America was filled with great expectations and we lived our lives to the fullest. Sandy was no exception. She was a carefree, fun-loving girl who fit right in with me and the rest of the "Pack."

Little did I realize then that she would go on to marry a physician and fellow Notre Dame Alumnus, would earn an MBA, would become a successful businesswoman, college professor, great mother, and most importantly, a true survivor.

Now she blesses us by becoming an author and giving us an account of some of our fun-filled "Glory Days."

I hope you enjoy reading the book as much as I have, and as much as we enjoyed living it.

Go Pack!

Paul Hornung
November 2003

(A poem written by me for THE GREEN BAY PACKERS
and given to them during Training Camp - 1962)

HELD AT BAY

It's time again to knuckle down

As CURFEW comes to PACKER Town,

No more weekends 'way from BAY,

But they will come another day.

The thought right now,

Forget the rest,

Is go to work and do your best.

Victory has a precious cost …

And most expensive when it's lost.

So, my friends, if things get tough,

Perhaps, you haven't done enough.

And that's the truth, *you know darn well…*

So let **me** know… I'll pray like hell!

By Sandy Young (Sullivan)

THE PREFACE

This book contains love stories about the Lombardi Green Bay Packers who I know best, and of whom I am so fond. In writing this book I want to share what I know about their love affair with football, each other, their families, and friends. They nurture a never-ending love affair with **GREEN BAY PACKER FANS** <u>everywhere</u>, who without question are the **<u>greatest</u>** fans in the world!

Inevitably, in telling these stories I give an account of my life and how it turned out okay, even though I did <u>NOT</u> get my wish and marry a football hero. My compliments to the women who did; the women who married their hero and had their dream come true. These <u>special</u> women stand in the shadow of their husband's glory, sacrifice much of their personal identity, contribute unselfishly to their husband's success, and stand patiently on the sidelines, waiting to help him. BRAVO! For all the women who secretly, or not so secretly, longed to marry a football hero… and did <u>NOT</u>… I understand how you feel… but don't forget to count your <u>blessings</u>!

I especially want to praise the <u>mothers</u> of football players who seldom get the credit they deserve. *<u>Many</u> **mothers** <u>are the source of their son's athletic ability… **not** the fathers.</u>* They are the ones who after a play, count the rising players, hoping their son is one of them. They offer coaching, support, encouragement, discipline, hope, example, love, and much more. They nurse his breaks and bruises, put him to bed at night, and wake him in the morning. They feed his ravenous appetite, wash his odoriferous clothing, and pray for the salvation of his soul. What would it be like without them? Not so great!

Most importantly this book is about **<u>LIVING</u>** and is meant to be a tribute to, and an example of, the indomitable creative strength of the FEMALE spirit…MINE! …and in thanks to my Creator for His abundant gifts.

Sandy Sullivan
Wisconsin-2004

GREEN BAY LOVE STORIES
AND
OTHER AFFAIRS

HOW DARE I WRITE ABOUT THIS?

When I was a young gal I wanted to marry a football hero! My friend, Ron Kramer, (Green Bay Packers 1957 & 1959-1964) never allows me to forget, nor does he ever stop ribbing me about the fact that although I tried hard, I never got my man. In younger years I thought it was dreadful I didn't get my wish, but with maturation, I learned the good Lord knew best, and I often thank my lucky stars… I was spared. I would have had a hard time being <u>only</u> a spectator, and not the leading performer in such a union. Not that all professional-sports marriages are subsequently structured, but had **I** married a star, we both would have experienced <u>identity</u> issues. Some may dispute this, but I believe Divine Providence may have rescued me before I bound myself to a "life-of-service" with an ego-maniac, who was <u>too</u>

1

<u>much</u> like me. The marriage probably would not have worked and the outcome may have been disastrous. We will never know! Regardless, the experiences which I encountered in quest of <u>my hero</u> qualify me to write this book.

Let me begin by stating a **TRUE FACT!** I LOVE PROFESSIONAL FOOTBALL PLAYERS! **<u>GREEN BAY PACKERS</u>** specifically! They are fast, sleek and clean. They are well-designed, give great performance and smell like new! It sounds like I am referring to a new sports car but here's what I mean! Most football players are physically drop-dead gorgeous, are well-disciplined, are usually smart, extremely exciting, and they smell good. Let me put it in other vernacular to be sure you catch my drift. Professional football players, especially Green Bay Packers (I'm partial to <u>them</u>), have physiques like Greek gods, are trained in self-control, are mentally-alert, are fairly well-educated (college grads), are extremely funny, are fun to be with, and they smell… squeaky <u>CLEAN</u>. Above all and most important to me, they usually have a <u>positive mental attitude</u> and they **<u>love women</u>.** When I was young I fooled myself into believing these were the only necessary requirements to make a man… a <u>man</u>.

The football players of the 1950's and 60's were every bit as "<u>HOT</u>" as the men of the present day, if not more so. It was very exciting in those days because "free sex and promiscuity" was a <u>new</u> thing… not the **norm** as it is today, when there are no surprises, and what you <u>don't</u> know about sex you can learn on the PLAYBOY or a DO-IT-YOURSELF channel. Remember, the 60's was the "dawning of the Age of Aquarius" and some women… were thrilled to experience this brave, new freedom, and celebrate our sexuality…and the football players <u>loved</u> it!

I have experienced many exciting times in my life; I have had a box seat on the finish line at Pimlico Race Track… been kissed in the U.S. Senate Dining Room by the late President of Egypt, Anwar Sadat… dined on the White House lawn with the President of the United States, Ronald Reagan, and been seated next to the late great crooner, Frank Sinatra in Vegas… to mention only a few. But I can honestly say… the most fun I <u>ever</u> had in my life… are the times I spent with my football

Sandy Sullivan

friends from Green Bay.

It began in 1961 in Milwaukee when I was 19 years old working as a model, and I was called for a job interview. The Green Bay Packers were looking for someone to work in their booth at the Milwaukee Sentinel Sports Show. The Packers were seeking exposure because they had recently added a new section of seats onto the stadium (6,000) and were <u>trying</u> to sell tickets. I'll jump ahead here and say I must have been <u>really good</u> at my job because the Packers are <u>now</u> sold out! (Just kidding!) I interviewed with Tom Miller, Assistant General Manager of the Packers under Vince Lombardi, and I was asked to work in a booth for 12 hours a day, for 9 days, with the promise of being paid $90 at week's end. WOW! Fantastic! Another girl got the job and I was <u>not</u> overly disappointed because I knew little about the Packers at the time, only that they were a "<u>not-so-good</u>" football team in Green Bay, and I had never been to Green Bay.

A few hours after arriving home from this interview, I received a call from Tom Miller saying the girl he had chosen to work for them had changed her mind, refusing the employment, and he asked if I, knowing I was his <u>second</u> choice, would accept the job. I accepted, but, I have often wondered what my life would have been like if I had said, "NO." It was a defining moment…a small decision which changed the course of my life… so much so I can say… that had I <u>not</u> taken that job in 1961, I would <u>not</u> have met my wonderful husband fifteen years later nor would my beautiful daughter, Kerry, have been born. Seeking your destiny requires taking chances and living at risk! (More about this later!)

In April I found myself at the Milwaukee Sentinal Sport Show, in the Green Bay Packer booth, giving out player's photos and showing a film of the previous year's Championship Game; the Packers losing the Western Division title to the Philadelphia Eagles in 1960. A few days into the session, Vince Lombardi came up to me in the booth grinning from ear to ear. I did <u>not</u> know who he was, and when Tom Miller introduced us, he asked Lombardi if he had any special instructions for me. Lombardi was charming! He had been watching me work the crowd from a distance and said I was doing a fabulous job.

Then he made a sweet, "corny" request. He said… he had a full back, a half back and a quarterback, and now, since he had me, would I come along… and be the "DRAWBACK?" At nineteen years of age I really didn't know what he meant, if anything, but I took him <u>seriously</u>… he would never know just how seriously!

I had a lot of fun showing the film, answering questions and giving out Packer pictures. By the end of the week I had reasonable knowledge of the subject of pro-football and the Packer organization. I took <u>special</u> interest in the players, memorizing their names and numbers. I became curious and quite intrigued when many <u>sharp-looking</u> gals approached and asked for pictures of Paul Hornung. I knew he was the Green Bay Packer's half back and was called the "Golden Boy." One day, two, little, African-American girls asked me for a picture of Paul, and I implied that they must want it to put on their *refrigerator* door. "Oh, <u>no</u>, Ma'am," they quickly corrected me, "we want it for our *bedroom*." <u>Wow, I had to meet **this** guy</u>!

Two weeks later I got my chance when I was Tea Room

(Lunch) modeling at Fazio's on Fifth, a popular restaurant in downtown Milwaukee. Frankie Fazio, one of the owners, brought me over to a table where Rocky Marciano, the champion heavy-weight boxer, and another man were sitting. "Let me introduce you to the fellows, Sandy. This is Rocky Marciano… and this is Paul Hornung." I barely gave Rocky the courtesy of a nod… but Paul?…WELL!… I couldn't believe my eyes! Here he was, in the flesh! Oh! My God! He was soooo CUTE! I stuttered, stammered, and finally told him about the two little girls who wanted his picture… for their bedrooms. He immediately asked me out and I immediately accepted. I thought he liked me a lot because he was supposed to speak at a banquet in another city that evening but called to cancel. He also invited me to be his guest at the Kentucky Derby coming up in May. Paul is a native of Louisville, KY and is an honorary Kentucky Colonel at the Derby. He said I could stay with his mother, at her house, if I was concerned about being properly chaperoned. SURE!!!

I refused the invitation saying my parents would not permit it, but the truth is …I wasn't very sure of myself and I lacked

the confidence I needed to accompany him. I made excuses to
myself saying my wardrobe and so on, would not be adequate
for such a grandiose event. Ironically, I married a man who
was <u>really</u> into horse racing and because of him, we frequently
went to Saratoga, NY in August, and watched the maiden races
of many, great thoroughbreds, and annually we attended the
Preakness in Maryland, and the Belmont Stakes in NYC… but
because the *opportunity* never came again, I have never been to
a Kentucky Derby… the <u>first</u> race of the Triple Crown.

All my life I have regretted my refusal of Paul's invitation.
If you ever have the opportunity to go somewhere… GO!
You only live once, and 40 years from now when you <u>won't</u>
be given the opportunity, or be asked to go anymore, you will
not be disappointed with yourself, have regrets, or feel badly
because you think you missed something. Taking advantage
of present opportunities… is one of the secrets to <u>living</u> a full
and happy life. Many people don't go and **<u>enjoy</u>** their youth,
and then they turn 40, or 50, or 60 and they feel they must have
missed something when they were young. They start to become
dissatisfied and begin to look <u>backwards</u> with longing. They

readily develop big-time problems. One of the things which made it easier for me to come back home and care for elderly family members in later years, is knowing I had not missed much of anything when I was young.

I recommend the **high-life** (within reason) to young people! As Auntie Mame said, "Life is a <u>banquet</u> and half the poor bastards are <u>starving</u> to death." You will never have a better chance to be foolish, make mistakes, and have fun than when you are young. There is a song which says, if you have the choice to "sit it out… or… dance"…….. by all means… **DANCE**! In sports they say, "Take the shot!" and "Go for it!" I say, "JUST <u>DO IT</u>!"

Back to my story!

I flipped over Paul Hornung! He was fun, exciting, good-looking, and **single**. Little did I know how many other women shared my sentiments.

(He was the catch of the Century!…The "GOLDEN BOY.")

Every time he came to Milwaukee he called me… at least… I <u>think</u> he did! He was probably in town many times when he didn't call. I didn't know it at the time, but among others, he was calling a beautiful girl who was President and Mamie Eisenhower's niece. When I finally found out about her I learned she was on the Milwaukee Social Register, and I thought I could not compete with her for Paul's attention…I felt inferior. Knowing Paul Hornung as I do today, I would have to say her social status did not mean a thing to him. He was a self-admitted "PLAYBOY" …and at the time, Paul was out to have a good time, and we were both "good-time" girls. Of course, both of us were vying for his attentions, as we should have been… he was everything a girl dreamed of!

Saturday May 13,1961

Chicken Broth   .15

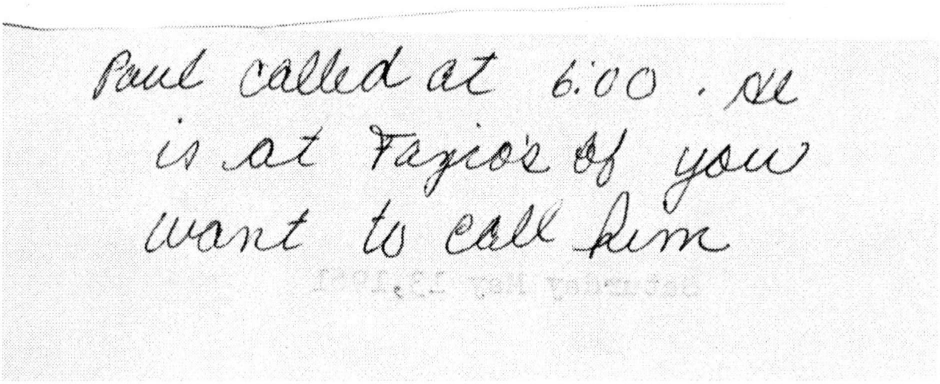

Paul called at 6:00 . He
is at Fazio's of you
want to call him

In the 1960's we did not have phone message pads. Messages were
written on the back of used paper. In this case, the operator used
cut-up strips of paper from our menu at the College Women's Club
in Milwaukee. I found this scrap of paper at the bottom of a drawer
which held many mementos and pictures of the Green Bay football
team of the 1960's.

1203 YOUNG SANDRA 11/30/650
WIS VS 6PM

Hotel
SCHROEDER
Milwaukee, Wis.

95810

Guest Ledger

MEMO.		DATE	EXPLANATION	CHARGES	CREDITS	BAL. DUE
	1	NOV 30-61	ROOM	★ 6.50		★ 6.50
	2	DEC-1-61	ROOM	★ 6.50		★ 13.00
	3					1.00
	4			— RMS.		
	5					14.00
	6					
	7					
	8					
	9					
	10					
	11					
	12					
	13					
	14					
	15					
	16					
	17					
	18					
	19					
	20					
	21					
	22					
	23					
	24					

PRESS OF THE NATIONAL CASH REGISTER CO. DAYTON OHIO   F325

SCHROEDER HOTELS IN MILWAUKEE, FOND DU LAC,
GREEN BAY, MADISON AND WAUSAU, WISCONSIN;
DULUTH, MINNESOTA; BENTON HARBOR, MICHIGAN.

LAST BALANCE IS AMOUNT DUE
BILLS ARE PAYABLE
WHEN PRESENTED

I have included this to give you an idea what the room rates were in 1961. Note: Room Service was $1.00 and there is no tax. One could stay two days in downtown Milwaukee at a good hotel for $13 and have a meal served in your room for $1.

This is the draft of a letter I wrote to Paul Hornung in November 1961 after I heard the news that he had been drafted into the U.S. Army.

13

Copy of a note from me to Paul at Fort Riley, Kansas just before the Championship Game on December 31, 1961.

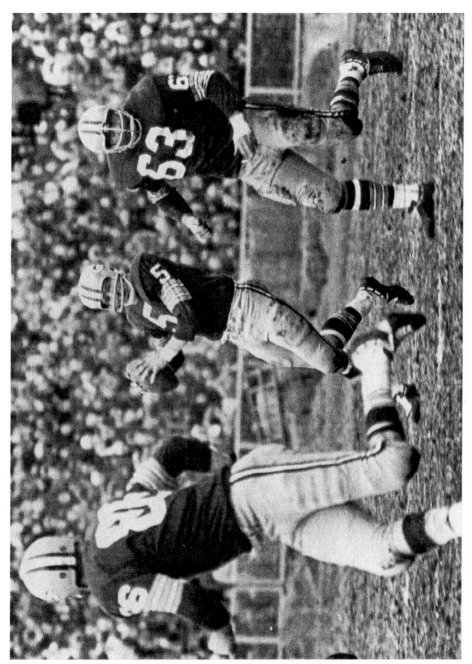

Colt/Packer game (1965) Paul Hornung contemplating a pass to Boyd Dowler #86. Fuzzy Thurston is the Left Guard #63. From the Collection of Vernon Biever (copyright)

One of the <u>first</u> Lambeau leaps. Note: Jim Ringo, Center #51 and Fuzzy Thurston, Left Guard #63, hold down the opposition. Gary Barnes OE #80 looks on. From the collection of Vernon Biever (copyright)

PAUL AND ME

    I quickly learned there are two things football players think about all the time… <u>FOOTBALL AND SEX</u>… and seldom in that order. One August weekend in 1961, some girlfriends and I drove to Green Bay for the game. I don't recall who the Packers were playing, and I was not as interested in the game as much as in the players. I did not have a formal date with Paul but he had not asked anyone <u>else</u> to be his date for the weekend, as I had told him I was coming and he had arranged tickets for all of us. As luck would have it, on Friday night most of the players could be found partying at a great, little, Green Bay saloon called Speed's. When I arrived I found Paul in the noisy crowd, and he told me he had to leave soon because there was a curfew at 11:00 P.M. It was during the pre-season and the

17

team was still in training camp staying at Sensenbrenner Hall on St. Norbert's College Campus. He was very attentive and told me he wanted to see me later, but first, Lombardi would be doing a bed-check around 11:30 P.M. to make sure the players were in their rooms, and he <u>had</u> to be there. He said as soon as it was safe for him to sneak out, he would call me. I stayed at Speed's and partied with my friends until mid-night, and then went back to the Downtowner Motel where we were staying, and waited for my call from the "Golden Boy." I promptly fell asleep, and finally, at 5:30 A.M. the telephone rang… and it was Paul. My girlfriends had a difficult time waking me, but when I came to… Paul told me to meet him in the parking lot behind the Downtowner. I was still in my clothes from the night before but I looked fine. Apparently, I had not moved a muscle waiting for him while I slept, so I primped my hair, brushed my teeth, gargled, and walked out into the early morning sunlight. ***WOW!*** There he was! My heart jumped right out of my chest and landed on my sleeve. He was leaning against his car… I think it was a Corvette. His golden hair was glistening in the sunlight and it was so bright, it hurt my eyes. He had on a cream-colored sweater with the initials "PH" embroidered on the left side, and he sported a smile which could have melted an iceberg.

"Hi! Where are we going?" I asked shyly. He hugged and kissed me, and said, "Honey, we're going over to the Northland Hotel. You're gonna' wait in the car... I'll go in and get us a room. Then I'll come out to get you, and we'll go upstairs and make love." THUMP! THUMP! THUMP! I felt a thrill go through me from the tip of my toes... to the top of my head. My blood pressure must have risen a hundred points, and even if I had wanted to say "NO," I was incapable of it. The excitement was unbelievable!

A few minutes later, Paul came scurrying out of the Northland. He said, "Honey, we have a slight change in plans!" "What's the matter?" I gulped, afraid our encounter was in jeopardy. "There's a bunch of coaches sitting in the lobby of the hotel. I can't take you through the lobby. Here's what I want you to do." We drove around to the back of the hotel and Paul pointed to an outside fire escape which looked like it had been there for a hundred years, and probably had. He said, "I'll pull it down so you can get on the stairs. You climb up the fire escape to the fifth floor. I'll go back in through the lobby and take the elevator to the fifth floor. I'll open the fire door from the inside and meet you there... OKAY?"

Well, now! I am all for thrills and exciting times but <u>this</u> was not in the travel brochure I had read. But, My Lord! It was Paul Hornung. I meekly whispered, "_{Okay}!" (*A little voice inside me said, "<u>Hey</u>, get with the program! You may never have an <u>opportunity</u> like this again.*") I questioned myself...eh...eh... had I mentioned that I'm deathly afraid of heights? ("*Don't tell him <u>that</u>! ... **<u>Just do it</u>!***") ...so up I went!

By the time I reached the fifth floor I was really scared. We "<u>dolled</u>" up in those days, and I had on a full-skirted dress, a lot like Marilyn Monroe had on in "The Seven Year Itch," when the air blew her dress up over her head. I had on three-inch, spike, high-heeled shoes, and my brand-new heels were going through the rungs of the fire escape. My dress and hair were blowing wildly in the wind and I was shaking! To top it off, I was clutching my hand bag. I could hear Paul's efforts on the other side of the door as he rammed it several times. It must have been painted-shut so he put all of his body weight into it. Bang… bang… **BANG**! (*He must have been in a hurry!*) Suddenly the door flew open …the wind caught it… and it hit me hard on my shoulder. Paul grabbed me before I went over the side.

Truly, I have <u>no</u> memory of going to a room and making love with <u>Paul Hornung</u>, although I must have! How could I <u>forget</u> something like that? But I can promise this … for as long as I live … <u>I will **never** forget that fire escape</u>!

I saw Paul Hornung at Ray Nitschke's funeral and reminded him of the incident but I don't believe he remembered. (*He's getting older, you know*!) After the funeral services some of us met at the Spot, a wonderful Green Bay, eating and drinking establishment; Ron Kramer, Boyd Dowler, Howard Ferguson, Paul, and me. (Kind of like old times!) When I told the story I built it up to a crescendo… and ended by asking, "…and do you know what, Pauly?" "What?" he asked, grinning eagerly. "All that effort… and you weren't that good!" Of course I absolutely <u>had</u> to say it, and his buddies… roared.

21

Friends, it must <u>always</u> be said that Paul Hornung is a good sport. The very best! He shrugged his shoulders, laughed with the rest of us, and accepted my <u>little dig</u> graciously. As he was leaving he winked and smiled at me, but then why wouldn't he? After all… **<u>I'm a good sport, too!</u>**

THE ORIGINALS

Before the Lombardi Packers, there were other crazy, fun-loving fellows, whose names are printed on the pages of Packer history, and they were every bit as <u>colorful</u> as the <u>Lombardi Legends</u>. You will see some of their names on the inside walls of Lambeau Field (Pro-Football - <u>Hall of Fame Members Only</u>), and the next time you attend a game in Green Bay you will know something about them.

LAMBEAU

Of course, for the first 31 years or so, there was Earl "Curly" Lambeau (Green Bay Packers 1919-1949), the founder of the team…the guy who started it all. Curly was a charming fellow with an abundance of <u>vision</u>, and who all of his life had a real <u>love affair</u> with football. He was a risk-taker, and in his earlier days, I am told he was a rogue. I'll bet he would be amazed to see the results of his dream for the Green Bay Packers. When Paul Hornung played at Green Bay, Curly Lambeau was still, very much alive, and I can remember times when I was dating Paul, Curly would invite Paul to spend time with him at his Summer home in Fish Creek, Door County, Wisconsin. They liked each other and I'll bet Curly saw <u>himself</u> in the young, blonde, curly-haired Hornung. Both had attended Notre Dame and both were "playboys" at heart. Both loved the <u>young</u> ladies, and many of the young ladies loved them. As Curly grew older his desire for beautiful <u>young</u> women did not subside… and then…along came Mary Jane. There is no doubt in my mind… theirs is a real <u>love</u> story.

Mary Jane Van Duyse was a beauty queen who grew up in Sturgeon Bay, a town near Fish Creek. She was the National Baton Twirling Champion and the World's Most Famous Drum Majorette, and because of her ability to entertain and rally a crowd, Vince Lombardi asked her to organize a cheerleading squad to represent his newly-appointed team, the Green Bay Packers. (1959-61) A year or so before, Mary Jane was twirling at Chicago's Wrigley Field with the Packer Band, and while doing a difficult, tricky routine… a cartwheel with a high toss in the air… she <u>missed</u> the catch. Determined she could get it right, she attempted it a second time and succeeded. The next day in the newspaper, an admiring Chicago Tribune reporter dubbed her "The Packer's **Golden Girl**" and the name stuck! Eventually the Packer cheerleaders, which Mary Jane established, would become known as the **Golden Girls**.

Fritz Van Duyse, Mary Jane's brother, introduced her to Curly Lambeau at a local restaurant, and the twirling beauty took an <u>immediate</u> liking to Curly. He was appealing… intelligent, distinguished, and a heck of a lot of fun, plus, they

25

had a lot in common as both worked for the Packers. He treated her like she was a "little girl" and <u>always</u> called her "Champ." He told her he called her this because of her Baton Twirling Championships and her love of athletics; golf, tennis, and swimming.

Curly often stopped by the Van Duyse house in Sturgeon Bay where Mary Jane resided with her parents, and he also began visiting the Golden Girl rehearsals, offering suggestions, but more intent on seeing Mary Jane. To this day the girls on the cheerleading squad often talk about those visits from Curly, and remember how he took publicity photos and encouraged them. Many say they took his being there for granted, not realizing his importance or the magnitude of the Packer dynasty... which was to come. Curly was excited over the new, nationally-popular, dance craze, "THE TWIST," and he helped Mary Jane and the Golden Girls incorporate it into a routine which was later performed on the field during the games, and also in a movie.

Gradually he endeared himself to her family, often visiting

her parents, even when she wasn't home. One evening he told <u>them</u> he <u>loved</u> her and wanted to <u>marry</u> her. He knew her parents were concerned about their age difference, and he then cited the similar age difference between Bing Crosby and Kathryn Grant. Curly said that "The Crosby's" had worked it out… and so could he and Mary Jane. To add more negatives to the relationship, Curly had been divorced quite a few times, and he guessed the strict-Catholic Van Duyse family would object to their marriage. However, he vowed he would resolve all of the problems. When told of this conversation with her parents, Mary Jane wavered… she had a budding career and was busy with her work… she didn't know what to think about his intentions.

Thanks to Marie Lombardi, Vince's wife, Mary Jane was asked to perform at the Pro-Bowl in Los Angeles in 1965. For Mary Jane, it was the thrill of a lifetime! She was staying at the home of friends in Los Angeles, and was surprised when Curly called and offered to take her to Mass on Sunday. While they were in church, he took a small box from his jacket pocket and gave her a diamond ring, asking her to marry him. She <u>loved</u>

him, but hesitated… "Curly, remember all the talks we've had about this… I can't accept." In return he said, "Look, you keep the ring until we can get married!" And upon his insistence, Mary Jane kept the ring. Only her parents and family knew about the ring and the proposal, and Curly was hopeful! He stayed in California for the rest of the winter months, and when he came back to Door County in May, he planned a special dinner for just the two of them. When he went to her home to pick her up, he drove into the driveway and saw her father mowing the front lawn. An excited Curly jumped out of the car and said, "Fritz! Let me help you!" Her father said "NO!" but Curly grabbed the lawn mower and started showing how he could do "THE TWIST" while mowing the lawn. Mary Jane had been watching them, enjoying the scene from the front porch. A moment later she went inside and then heard her father cry-out. While they were clowning around, Curly had suddenly fallen backwards into her father's arms. Her father held Curly's head in his lap as Mary Jane ran to them. She cried, "Curly! Curly! I love you… I love you." Her mother phoned a doctor, the rescue squad, and a priest. He died… and Mary Jane held him in her arms until they came for him.

Had the timing been different or had she decided differently, Mary Jane Van Duyse, <u>easily</u>, could have become Mary Jane Lambeau… Mrs. Curly Lambeau. As it turns out she is remembered as the Packer's original, "<u>Golden Girl</u>."

Don't cry! There's a happy ending to the sad love story of Mary Jane and Curly. A short time later she met a wonderful fellow named Bill Sorgel and married him. One day Bill asked Mary Jane if he could borrow the diamond ring Curly had given her. A few days later he presented her with his <u>own</u> diamond ring, but had included in the setting the diamond which Curly Lambeau had given. Bill not only wanted her to have <u>his</u> diamond, but believed she should have Curly's diamond as well. He felt it was appropriate for her to be <u>often</u> reminded of the love of this special man. To this day Mary Jane wears the ring and looks at it to remind her of Curly, and of course, her beloved husband, Bill.

When I was young I found this poem in a women's magazine and memorized it. It fits in… right here:

Some are mentioned in <u>Who's Who</u>

because of <u>what their husbands do</u>.

And some, twice <u>lucky, miss</u> the glare

of public life's unceasing stare…

And, nonetheless, have come to be…

<u>endowed with immortality.</u>

Thus, lovely Sally, wed and true,

knew neighbor, George, (Washington) adored her, too.

And Mary Owen gave up with pride,

the chance to be Abe Lincoln's bride.

So, ladies fair, with "Yes" be slow…

<u>Your **fame** may also rest in "**NO**."</u>

…………

BLOOD

Another person whose name you will see in Lambeau field, and who is in the Professional Football Hall of Fame, is John "Blood" McNally. (Green Bay Packers 1929-1933 and 1935-1936, HOF 1963) John McNally, like Curly Lambeau, attended Notre Dame for a <u>little</u> while. (Did you know the University of Notre Dame has given more football players to the Packer organization than any other school? Good Trivia!) One Saint Patrick's Day, while attending Notre Dame, John McNally got carried away. Literally! He and a buddy got on a motorcycle, drove out of South Bend, and never returned. (*It sounds like something I would do…what am I saying?… something I HAVE done! A man after my own heart*!) After skipping out of school at Notre Dame, John McNally enrolled himself in St. John's University in Minneapolis, where he played football on Saturdays. At the time, Minneapolis had a professional football team named the Liberties. McNally wanted to play for <u>them</u>, <u>also</u>, but one was not allowed to play on a college team and a

31

professional team at the same time. In order to play for both, he had to somehow disguise his identity. This was around 1925 and there was a movie starring Rudolph Valentino playing in the theatres. McNally and a buddy saw the movie title on a marquee and decided to assume the name of the movie, "Blood and Sand." I don't know what became of "<u>Sand</u>," but I do know what happened to "<u>Blood</u>." John "Blood" McNally became one of the greatest halfbacks in the history of the National Football League, and he used the name "<u>Johnny Blood</u>" to play pro-ball. Johnny Blood was also known as the "Vagabond Halfback."

History tells us Johnny Blood played his best when the situation was the most difficult…when the pressure was really on. That's the time he could be counted on to accomplish the "almost" impossible. I am reminded of Vince Lombardi's similar praise of Boyd Dowler's performances in the book, **<u>Vince Lombardi On Football</u> (1973).** Lombardi says, "Boyd Dowler <u>never</u> <u>received</u> the national publicity that he deserved as one of the great receivers. He was always <u>best</u> in our <u>championship games</u>." (*Lombardi said, Boyd always "hung on to the ball."*) I guess that's when it counts most, right? Can we

safely say Boyd and Blood are both dependable fellows? Sure
we can… two of a kind!

Johnny Blood was a legend unto himself and he signed
his love letters with his own blood. Well why not? What a
romantic! (*I never even received an **ink**-written letter from Paul
Hornung. Gee! Some guys just don't have a romantic flare!*)
It is said… Johnny Blood was dashing, daring, and full of the
devil. I heard that one time he had been out all night, and did
not want to get fined by the coach, Curly Lambeau. He had
forgotten the key to his fifth floor room, and he couldn't go to
the desk and ask for a key because Curly was sitting in the hotel
lobby with some of the coaches. (*Sound familiar?*) Well, Johnny
Blood did <u>not</u> climb the fire-escape to the fifth floor, as I did
under the instructions of Mr. Hornung. However, he did locate
a teammate who had a room on the sixth floor, almost directly
<u>across</u> from his room. By "across" I mean <u>across</u> a courtyard,
six stories below. It was a 12-foot jump, but Johnny Blood
leaped from the sixth floor window of his teammate's room, to
the fifth floor window of his own room, avoiding a fine from
Curly. (*Wow! Daring!*) I am certainly relieved Paul Hornung

didn't make me try this feat to get to the fifth floor… but one never knows… some guys will try anything to get "you-know-what." Incidentally, this is not recommended to be tried by my readers.

Look closely! You will find a picture which I took of John Blood McNally in 1972 in Lambeau Field. I was fortunate to meet him before he died (1985). (*It's probably a good thing that I didn't know him when I was young, or, I would have gotten into more trouble than I did!*)

BUCKETS

There was another member of the team (circa. 1935), who became one of my best friends... Charles (Buckets) Goldenberg. (Green Bay Packers 1933-1945) Sometimes, when John Madden announces a Monday Night game for Green Bay, he brings up the name of Buckets Goldenberg. I don't know why, but he often mentions him. (*John, I think you like the sound of his name*!) The story goes that Buckets got his name because of the way he caught the football... he scooped it up, like he was catching it in a bucket. He owned a restaurant which he called "Pappy's" in the Bayshore Shopping Center. Bayshore is a suburb just north of Milwaukee, and I met him there while modeling. Buckets was a <u>second</u> father to me, and I especially loved him because he thought Paul Hornung and I would make an excellent couple. He even told me our Zodiac signs were <u>meant</u> for each other. Apparently he had read somewhere that Taurus people (ME) and Capricorn people (PAUL), are perfectly matched in the stars. (*Cool!*) I think he actually told

35

Curly Lambeau about me and suggested Curly put in a good word to Paul for me. I surmised this because strangely, Paul once asked me how I <u>knew</u> Curly, and I did not. Buckets denied telling Curly about me, but he smiled when he denied it.

Buckets liked me and looked out for me… like when I moved for about the 10th time in one year… Buckets let me borrow his car for each move. Something like this means a lot to a kid without means, and without a car. My Mom and Dad met him and I can remember them telling him how much they appreciated his kindness to me. Many years later I was in Milwaukee with my parents and my new husband, Matt Sullivan. Dan Currie had driven up from Chicago to meet us, and we were at the bar in the Milwaukee Inn, when suddenly, in walked my old friend, Buckets. When I told my husband who he was, my husband remembered the story about my 21st Birthday party which Buckets had given me, and reached to shake his hand. Buckets gave my husband a hug! *Honestly*! I am sure Buckets was pleased I had met and married this special man. The year had to be about 1979-1980, and Buckets died in 1986, so I am pleased to have seen him again and been able to express my gratitude to him.

RE: The 21ˢᵗ Birthday Party

When I was about to turn 21 years old, Buckets decided
I should have a SUPER DUPER 21ˢᵗ Birthday party. I think
the plans for this event evolved because he was relieved I was
finally turning 21, and that it would now be <u>legal</u> for me to
drink at his bar and restaurant. Up to this point I had probably
consumed 25 gallons of booze there, illegally. I recall I loved to
drink a Blackberry Brandy Alexander made with ice cream! His
bartender spoiled me, and I had to watch my weight because of
this luxury. With the help of his wife, Marian, he organized my
birthday party at an Italian restaurant on the upper north side of
Milwaukee at Prospect and Farwell. He arranged for the Chef
to prepare an 11-course Italian Dinner in my honor, and invited
many of his and my friends. It was absolutely **grand**! Before
the dinner he told me there were four things a young lady needs
to be given on her 21ˢᵗ Birthday; a new dress, flowers, a bottle
of fine champagne, and a party. Buckets provided all four, and
he picked me up at my place in a limousine. I will never forget
the special attention I was given that evening. What a wonderful

treat…one I will remember all my life!

• • • • • • • • • •

HUTSON

I met the other fellow whose name is on the wall in
Lambeau Field, while modeling at Pappy's restaurant. Buckets
introduced me to a man who was having lunch by the name
of Don Hutson. (Green Bay Packers 1935-1945, HOF 1963)
After I finished work, we all sat around talking and enjoying a
few drinks. When late afternoon rolled around it was time for
Don Hutson to leave and drive home. He had to go right by my
house on West Wells Street, so Buckets asked him to give me a
ride to my apartment. We engaged in pleasant conversation and
when we arrived at my door, he turned and casually asked me if
I wanted to go to bed with him. Well, at the time, I was 20 years
old and he was about 50. *Gee*! I thought he was a relic from
the Stone Ages, and besides, couldn't he tell, I was in love with
Paul Hornung. I said, "NO!" and he said, "OK!" …and that was
that. How wonderful… a man who could easily take "No" for
an answer. He was in Sales… so he was probably conditioned
to hearing the word "NO." Nevertheless, I think I was a little

flattered to be asked by this famous football player. Please, dear reader, please, remember… I was young and dumb… I thought this was a compliment. I told Buckets about the incident and probably should <u>not</u> have, because a mutual friend told me that Buckets called-up Don Hutson and gave him <u>HELL</u>. What a guy… I mean Buckets. He was the <u>real</u>, football hero!

Mary Jane Van Duyse, the Original Packer Golden Girl, dazzles the
Green Bay fans

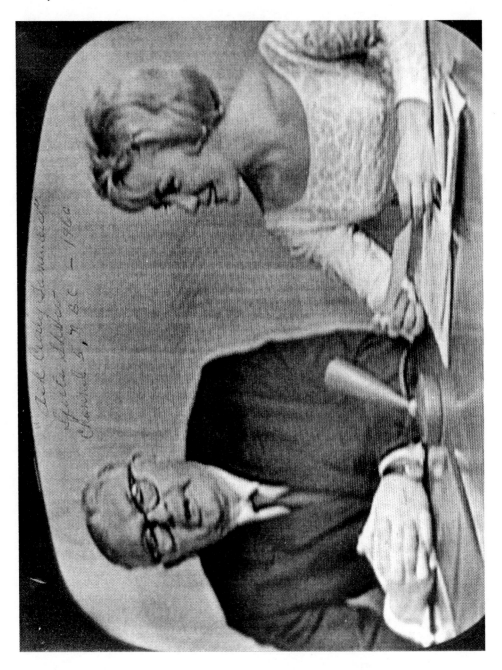

Curly Lambeau and Mary Jane Van Duyse (Sorgel) on the "Ask
Curly Lambeau" Sports Show   NBC-Channel 5 (1960)

(From left to right) Dan Currie (GB 1958-1964),Gale Gillingham
(GB 1966-1976), <u>JOHN "BLOOD"MCNALLY</u> (GB 1929-1936) and
Francis Peay (GB 1968-1972). (Photo taken by the author, Alumni
Weekend, Lambeau Field, 1972)

This is me at my 21st Birthday Party, May 10,1962

(From left to right) My friends: Don Kindt, star of University of
Wisconsin football and the NFL Chicago Bears, Grace Bradley,
Buckets Goldenberg, and me at the bar just before my party. Buckets
is smiling because I can drink legally. (5/10/1962)

Enjoying myself with my friends, Don Kindt and Buckets
Goldenberg. Note: See the orchid Buckets bought for me near his
left hand. It is pinned to my evening bag." (5/10/1962)

This is one of the publicity photos from my portfolio when I was modeling in Milwaukee and dating Paul Hornung (Age 20) Photo by Peter Kuluras - Milwaukee, WI (1961)

ENTER: DAPPER DAN

The Northland Hotel was in the middle of downtown, and I usually stayed there when I went to Green Bay. The reason being… if you asked for a room on the west side of the building you had a "birds-eye" view of the Lyric Lounge across the street, and I liked this "look-out" because I could see the people (the players), coming and going, in and out of the Lyric.

One evening when I was <u>supposed</u> to hear from <u>him</u>… <u>Paul</u> got tied up in a meeting… or <u>so he said</u>. He didn't come to the hotel but sent his friend and teammate for me. While I was watching the popular television program, "Leave It To Beaver," someone knocked on the door and when I opened it, I thought I had died and gone to heaven… I was stunned! I thought I was

49

seeing a <u>vision!</u> Before me… stood the <u>most</u> <u>handsome</u> man I had ever laid eyes on. SSSSSSeriously! I'm talking "**movie-star**" handsome. My jaw dropped, I must have looked like a fool, and he bashfully said, "Hello, I'm Dan Currie. Paul sent me!" (Green Bay Packers 1958-1964) I could tell we liked each other the moment we saw each other. Always have, always will! This much is for <u>sure</u> … I am, absolutely, positive, I liked him. **WOW**! He was sooo cute! After a little conversation, he invited me to dinner in the Northland Hotel Dining Room, and he bought me a Salisbury steak with all the trimmings; the cost of the dinner was $1. How's that for a memory? When one meets a fellow who looks like Dan, I guarantee you remember every detail of the first meeting.

I had no idea that in time to come I would live with this man for four years, our friendship would span over forty years, and knowing him would result in the most important events of my life; marriage to my wonderful husband, and then the birth of my favorite person on earth, my little girl. But this was not to happen right away. Patience!!! (*Unfortunately, not one of my virtues!*)

I soon learned Dan Currie was married and had a bunch of kids. That made him "off limits" for me. Darn it! However, I would be less than honest if I said I did not <u>secretly</u> wish he were single. If he <u>had</u> been single I would have been all over him, like flies on honey. As it was… I was all over him anyhow, in a manner of speaking. I wanted to be with him as much as possible, if for no other reason than to <u>stare</u> at him. He was so beautiful! I immediately "glommed-on" to him, and I had a hard time <u>not</u> falling for him. He was drop-dead gorgeous, and so much fun to be with. To top it off, he was a "nice" guy. He was an impeccable dresser, plus, he could sing like a pro… and he was always singing to me or my girlfriends…"in the wee, small hours of the morning…when the whole, wide world is fast asleep…you lay awake and think about the girl…and never-ever think of counting sheep." SIGH! One would have to be in a <u>coma</u> not to want <u>him</u>.

Dan Currie was this great, big, gorgeous man, who laughed a lot, and to make him even <u>more</u> interesting, he was a <u>top-notch</u> football player. He had been an All-American Football

51

Star at Michigan State University. By some group, he had been voted to have the best hands in 100 years of Big Ten Football. I think later…Dick Butkus beat him for this honor. (Trivia: (*My opinion*) Do you know the Center must have the most <u>accurate</u> hands on a football team? Put that in your little book of facts to use when you're with the gang watching a game. You might surprise someone… Or, you'll get into a disagreement if they do not concur, but stick to your guns because it's true. If they dispute you and say it is the quarterback… ask them who gives the ball to the quarterback.)

Dan had been given the All-American trophy/award on the Sunday night, nationally-televised, Ed Sullivan Show. The trophy reads as follows: "Presented to Daniel Currie, Michigan State University. Selected by the All America Board of the American Football Coaches Association as the Outstanding Player of the Year." (See photo) To top <u>this</u> off, he was the Number One NFL Draft Choice in 1958. Pretty impressive… if you ask me!

When my girlfriends and I were coming to Green Bay, it

got so we depended on Dan to get us rooms and tickets, and of course, to meet us at Speed's to party. He always made time to be with us... his family was back in Detroit, so, he had the opportunity to spend time with friends and fans... but I think at times he was a little lonely.

I remember one time when we (my girlfriends and I) stayed for a couple extra days at the Northland. I called Dan ahead of time and he reserved a suite of rooms for us. The reservation was in my name so I paid the bill, but, I don't remember checking out. About a month later, I ran into Dan at the King's X, a bar and restaurant in Green Bay. When he saw me he started to roar with laughter. I asked what was so funny and he lowered his head and said my name in a deep voice... slowly and solemnly ..."S-a-n-d-r-a." Then, he opened his wallet and pulled out the check written by me to pay for the suite of rooms. He handed it to me, saying he had covered it. When I perused the check I could not believe I had written it. When I wrote it I must have been "slightly?" inebriated. Illegible scribbling was all over it... and I was embarrassed! Dan kept on laughing. At first I didn't understand, and then he explained saying that since he had initially made the reservation at the Northland, the hotel's manager called him about the check. Apparently, it was so <u>bad</u> the bank wouldn't honor it and had returned it to the hotel. It was a starter check and did not have my name and address printed on it, and no one could figure out my name, so they called Dan… at the Packer office no less. The hotel manager asked Dan to cover the hotel charges and he did. Yes, Sir! Dan Currie did <u>this</u> for me. The check amounted to approximately $55. …and that doesn't sound like much money, but at today's rate of exchange it would be over $500. He would not let me reimburse him for the money. (*Thanks, Danny!)* I'll bet Dan has forgotten all about this. Am I right?

Another weekend in October we had stayed in Green Bay an extra day or so, looking for fun; we didn't go <u>immediately</u> back to Milwaukee after the game. On Wednesday morning as my girlfriends and I were leaving with our suitcases, we passed a room in the hotel on the same floor as our room. In those days there were transoms (a window or shutter-like panel over a door) for the circulation of air. There was no air-conditioning in the Northland Hotel, and as we passed the room, we could

easily hear Dan in his bathroom singing at the top of his lungs.
We giggled as we passed; it was delightful to hear him sound
so happy. I was surprised he was in the hotel and wondered
why he was there because he and Paul Hornung had gone to
New York City right after the game on Sunday. Paul had been
hired to shoot a soap commercial and had asked Dan to go with
him. Dan was concerned and said he needed permission from
Lombardi to go, but Paul told him not to worry… he would
clear the trip with Vince. While Lombardi was surrounded
by people and the press after the game, Paul quickly went up
to him and mumbled that Dan was going with him to New
York. Being pre-occupied, Lombardi probably never heard or
understood what was said. He barked, "Okay, but be back in
time for practice on Tuesday!" AND, the two of them were
off to the "Big Apple." Oh, boy! While Paul was shooting
the commercial, Dan went to Yankee Stadium to see one of
the games of the World Series. There were 66,606 people in
attendance that afternoon, and Dan Currie. The Yankees played
San Francisco, and Juan Marichal rewarded the crowd with
a magnificent pitching performance, and San Francisco beat
New York, 7-3. That was certainly tame enough! Right? Right!

Then, like dutiful young men, they went to the airport to catch their plane to return to Green Bay in time for Tuesday practice, but… (*Oh, no!*) the airport was fogged in! Because of that <u>darn</u> fog they had to stay in NYC an extra night. Poor kids! They spent the evening doing **the twist** at the Peppermint Lounge; supposedly, the <u>hottest</u> night spot in the country. (*Oh …come on! They had to go somewhere to get out of the rain.*) Tuesday morning practice came…and no Paul …and no Dan. Lombardi was furious! On Wednesday morning they were back and all I could ascertain is that Dan was very happy and singing, and I'll bet that Paul, wherever he was, was singing, too!

I still had a crush on Paul Hornung, but after meeting Dan Currie, Paul Hornung, for many reasons, didn't look <u>quite</u> as good to me.

There was a photo in the newspaper of Dan on his hands and knees with folded hands, praying for a win on December 31st. He looked like an angel so I wrote him a note about it and wished him good luck in the Championship game

Dan is presented the All-America Award by Michigan State
University Head Football Coach, Duffy Dougherty. (1957)
Photographic Laboratory, Michigan State University Information
Services, Negative # 19451-1, from the personal collection of Dan
Currie with permission.

Dan Currie receiving the All America Award from Ed Sullivan on the
Ed Sullivan Show, circa January 1958. From the personal collection
of Dan Currie with permission.

Dan Currie, and U.S. Vice-President, Richard M. Nixon, on the
campaign trail in East Lansing, Michigan (1956-57) From the
personal collection of Dan Currie with permission

Vince Lombardi

THE MAN WHO MADE THE GREEN BAY PACKERS GO

Lombardi's Green Bay players carried him off the field after the Packers clinched the Western Division title.

(From left to right) Gary Knalfelc #84, Dan Currie #58 holding Vince Lombardi, Jesse Whittenton #46 also holding Lombardi and Jerry Kramer #64 pointing to Lombardi. In far background, see Max McGee's eyes and part of Emlen Tunnell's face. (see directly behind Kramer) Lombardi brought Emlen with him from the New York Giants. He played for Green Bay from 1959-1961 and was one of the oldest players retiring at age 39-40. He played 13 years in the NFL and was inducted into the Pro-Football Hall of Fame in 1967. From Sports magazine (Dec. 1961) and from the personal collection of Dan Currie with permission

Dan
Currie

Publicity photo of (movie-star-handsome) Dapper Dan Currie in Los Angeles in 1965. Note the Rams ring, the white shirt and tie, and the always-shined shoes.

Two young cuties!!! Jerry Kramer and Dan Currie at Green Bay Training Camp (1959) (From the collection of Dan Currie with permission)

MAXI, THE TAXI

As time went on I began going to Green Bay more frequently; sometimes by invitation from Paul, and other times with a bunch of girlfriends from Milwaukee. It was during one of the **girlfriend** trips that I met Max McGee. (Green Bay Packers 1954 1957-1967) No story should ever be told about Paul Hornung which does not include Max McGee. They are, and always will be, very close friends, and at the time they were roommates. Often referred to as the "<u>girlfriends</u>," "**<u>Maxine and Pauline</u>**," they have always loved each other, and have had a lot of fun together. Lombardi scolded them one day during practice calling them "Prima Donnas," to which Max is supposed to have responded, "That's right, Coach... he's <u>Primo</u>, and ... I'm <u>Donna</u>." You probably had to be there ... but I'm sure you get the picture.

Well… one evening I went to Speed's with my girlfriends, and a big fellow came in and started dancing **the twist** with me. The "PEPPERMINT TWIST" and Chubby Checker were a big hit then… and the entire nation was twisting. As I said, in New York City the Peppermint Lounge was gaining fame because of the dance craze. I knew this fellow twisting with me was Max McGee. He asked my name and when I told him "Sandy," he acknowledged me with an all-knowing grin. Did Hornung kiss and tell? Of course he did!

I recall congratulating Max on his recent marriage to the famous pro-golfer, Doug Sanders' ex-wife, a gorgeous blonde named B. He did not seem thrilled to be a groom, and I could tell from his comments the marriage was already rocky, and it was only a few months old. Ron Kramer wants me to add this… every time he (Ron) sees Doug Sanders in Florida he inquires, "How do you like Green Bay, Doug?" He yells back, "I love 'em. They helped me get that woman off my payroll!" Apparently, Doug is appreciative to Max for relieving him of the marital responsibility of supporting B. When B divorced Max, she was required by law to wait until Max set foot in the State of Florida before he could be served with divorce papers. Apparently this happened right before a Dolphin-Green Bay game in Miami. Ouch! There are two sides to every story… I don't know her side, so, I will not comment further.

I have a very, good-looking, **blonde** girlfriend named Grace L. and Max McGee liked her (mostly, because she was <u>blonde</u>) and invited her to many games in Green Bay. Grace, being a sweetheart, would never go unless she could bring me along… and Max always agreed. He didn't care if I was with them. I was the kid who got to tag along… and I had a ball! I think Grace thought of me as her chaperone. Oh, brother! What a choice! She was pretty straight-laced, and as you recall… we were just coming out of the sexual, Dark Ages.

After the game, Grace and I waited by the Locker Room door for Max to appear. It was very exciting! Some of us would sigh, and our hearts would beat faster when the players appeared. Most every woman wanted to be seen with someone on the team. However, Grace was <u>not</u> impressed… and she couldn't have cared less. Her attitude temporarily intrigued Max, but after a time, his fascination of her wore off. He could get <u>nowhere</u> with her, and he finally stopped calling. (In my opinion, and to her credit, she was probably too straight-laced to date a pro-ballplayer) However, they dated for most of the season, and I had a great time while it lasted.

Back to my story-

After the game, we immediately headed to a worthwhile <u>watering-hole</u> where the party soon began. In the 1960's, the drug of choice was **<u>alcohol,</u>** and we single-handedly kept the Justerini and Brooks Scotch Company (J&B) in business. I thought it was a competition; I had to belly-up to the bar with the boys. I tried to keep up drink-for-drink and could for a time, but naturally, it was a losing battle. I <u>always</u> ended up having too much to drink. When it comes to drinking, though I hate to admit it, I <u>cannot</u> run with the "big dogs"… and painfully, after experiencing many hangovers, I have finally learned it is best for me to be "a porch dog." It never registered with me that... these fellow are top athletes in peak physical condition, and have just finished playing a professional football game... <u>winning</u> it! No wonder alcohol had so <u>little</u> effect on them... they were pumped! In my defense, I am no different than my fellow Packer fans who simply get caught up in the excitement of the moment and "party hardy." RIGHT?

To offer an example of my poor constitution and my over indulgence, I once said to Fuzzy Thurston, Green Bay's great left guard, that I couldn't figure out why I felt so terrible the next day after a bunch of us had partied the night before. I was dieting and I said, "Gee, I feel just awful and I only drank Rhine wine and seltzer." To which Fuzzy remarked, "Well, for Chrissake, Sandra, if you drink ten gallons of anything you're going to feel bad!"

When referring to Max McGee, please notice how I <u>emphasize</u> "**BLONDES.**" Max <u>always</u> went out with **blonde**s. He loved **blondes**... he adored **blondes.** At the time, he would probably not have been caught dead with a brunette, or a redhead. Therefore, it is not at all surprising... Hornung is a

blonde.

Max would delight us by telling of shaving cream fights in St. Norbert's Dorm, the strange "dork" sandwiches they made, and many of the inside stories about his teammates. I remember one story about a teammate whose name I cannot tell you. (Sorry!) Apparently, this fellow was making love to a girl in the Mississippi River at La Crosse, WI. Obviously he had his mind on other things, and was almost (s)ucked under by a huge freighter (ship) navigating the river. This same fellow narrowly escaped a husband's wrath by <u>quickly</u> scrambling out of a bedroom window. Unfortunately for him, he left his brand new shoes under her bed. But, he didn't get caught!

Max told a story about returning to his apartment one night with a young lady he did not know… very well. He had a sum of cash with him and decided it would be prudent to hide the money. For a hiding place, he chose the inside breast-pocket of a sports jacket which he hardly ever wore. A year or so later, he gave the jacket to a buddy. The following day the buddy approached Max and said, "Thanks for the jacket… but I don't think you wanted me to have <u>this</u>, or <u>did</u> you?" The friend handed over $3,000 in cash to Max. Max had forgotten all about the money and it's fortunate he'd given the jacket to a friend, and had not taken it to be cleaned.

Max has a delightful sense of humor, and a slow Texas way of delivering a punch line which is sure to catch you off guard, and put you in stitches. I am reminded of him on a radio show when the subject came up about a trainer with the Tampa Bay Bucs who was taking a bandage off a player's hand, and accidentally cut off the tip of the player's finger. In a slow, relaxed, rhythm, Max drawled, "That guy's lucky he didn't have a **groin** injury."

I enjoyed hearing of his continual bad luck with automobiles. He loved beautiful and sometimes impractical cars, but don't tell him I said so! (*He, also, loved beautiful and sometimes impractical females.*) Don't tell him I said that either. Convertibles in the 60's, and even now, are not extremely practical in Wisconsin's winter weather. But Max didn't care! He purchased a new Cadillac... and it must have been a convertible, and it was probably <u>red</u>. (**Blondes** look especially <u>fine</u> in **red, Cadillac convertibles!**) At a party Max felt he had had too much to drink, and he looked around for a teammate who was sober enough to drive his car home for him. He chose Nate Borden (Green Bay Packers 1955-1959) and gave Nate the keys. Unfortunately, Max did not realize Nate was drunker than he. Nate took the car, hit a patch of ice, and slid into the front window of a furniture store in downtown Green Bay. The sign above the window read something like…

"COME IN AND SEE OUR NEW WINTER LINE"

The big, bright, red Cadillac convertible sat right in the middle of the window. The Green Bay Press Gazette took a picture and put it in the paper the next day. I asked the Gazette to find the picture, if possible, and send it to me. I think they are still looking.

One hot August afternoon some of the boys were drinking in a bar in downtown Green Bay. Perhaps it was the Lyric Lounge? Paul, Max, and Ron Kramer lived together in a house they had rented. One of their "perks" was the generosity of a local dairy, which gave them free milk to drink. As they sat drinking booze, the milkman stuck his head in the door and asked if it would be all right to put the case of milk bottles (yes, "**BOTTLES**") in Max's Cadillac convertible, saving himself a trip to their house. Somebody yelled, "Sure, go ahead!" Late that evening Max piled into his car and drove home. For some reason he slammed on the brakes and the case of milk bottles broke. I don't think he even realized they were in his car. Anyhow, the next day, and maybe the day after that, and maybe the day after that, and so on …he didn't drive his Cadillac, but instead, rode to practice with Ron or Paul. It was very **HOT** that August!!! You know the rest of the story! Yep, had to get a new Caddy!

Max was out very late one night during the season. He shouldn't have been out after curfew. Lombardi was strict, imposing big fines for breaking it, and of course, Max didn't want to get caught and fined. On this particular evening his usual good luck was not with him. On his way home he had to cross a railroad track, and a night watchman on a railroad hand-car was pushing and pumping his way along the tracks. The railroad hand-car had no lights, so Max did not see it, and the hand-car collided into the side of Max's car. There are <u>few</u> secrets in Green Bay! Lombardi and the team were at practice the next morning and read <u>all about it</u> in the newspaper… Max was there for the **reading**, too! The <u>reading-out,</u> that is!

Ron Kramer tells a fun story about the two of them. The Packers were in Los Angeles for a game, and one morning Max told Ron he had a date with a lovely "Senorita" that evening, and had promised to take her dancing. Ron said, "Good for you! - What's wrong?" Max said he didn't know how to CHA, CHA, CHA. Kramer couldn't believe it! Here was one of the greatest and most natural athletes, and finest receivers of all time, and he didn't know how to… CHA, CHA, CHA??? How could this be? Ron said, "Come on, Buddy, don't worry. I'll show you how!" So they moved the beds apart to make room and started to dance in each other's arms <u>in their underwear</u>. They were doing really well until a maid opened the door. (What I wouldn't give to have a picture of that scene in this book.)

Max McGee is one of the most "laid" and "laid-back" persons I know. I have come to learn there is a definite correlation between "laid" and "laid-back." He is so calm and relaxed all the time. Amazing! Even though we like to kid around about Max, he always kept his wits about him, and he rarely became intoxicated, at least where it would show. When I think back on all the times I was with Max, he always seemed to be in complete control. Perhaps this is one of the reasons for his many successes. On the other hand, Ron Kramer claims I never saw him sober, and that is why I never knew he was drunk. Then again, I probably was not sober, so how in heck would I know!

Max can be very <u>quiet</u>, and sometimes I found myself standing next to him at a bar, feeling uncomfortable because I did not have anything to discuss with him. I told Dan Currie about this and he suggested I ask Max about his most recent trip to Las Vegas; inquire about his gambling luck! Holy Cow! I couldn't shut him up. At the time, I had little experience with the subject, but my question did the trick. I felt Max had at least enjoyed my company. Remember! If one wants to get someone's attention and encourage conversation, it is important to find out what it is that pushes their "starter button."

Obviously, Las Vegas is a "turn-on" for Max.

Not only was Max a successful athlete, but he has become a successful husband, father, commentator, businessman and philanthropist. A wonderful story about one of Max's business successes needs to be told. After football, Max and Fred "Fuzzy" Thurston (Green Bay Packers 1958-1967), along with a friend, Bill Martini, started the chain of restaurants called The Left End in Manitowoc, WI and The Left Guards throughout Wisconsin. They also had a restaurant in Minneapolis of which Max was in charge.

The story tells of another "receiver" named Bob Long (Green Bay Packers 1964-1967) who played a somewhat instrumental part in Max's monetary gains. Bob Long graduated from Wichita State University with a degree in Business Administration, and he came to Green Bay to play the wide receiver position but was seldom given the opportunity. In the line-up, he followed Max McGee, Boyd Dowler (Green Bay Packers 1959-1969) and Carroll Dale (Green Bay Packers 1967-1970). Lombardi sometimes let him start... and Bob Long always did well, but Lombardi told him he was holding him back because he felt he was too young. Lombardi said he was grooming him for later. "How much later?" concerned Long.

Bob Long is a go-getter! Though he was a superb athlete, he was also smart enough to realize he may not make it in pro-football given the present roster of the Green Bay team. He was eager for success! He had seen a new restaurant chain just starting up in his home state of Kansas, called PIZZA HUT. Bob went to the Pizza Hut headquarters and asked if he could buy the franchise rights for the State of Wisconsin. They said "Yes" and it would cost $20,000. He used his Super Bowl (1966) money which amounted to $15,000 and set out to raise the other $5,000 from his teammates.

Tommy Joe Crutcher (Green Bay Packers 1964-1967 & 1971-1972) had also seen the start-up of Pizza Hut in his home state of Texas, and agreed it was a great opportunity. Tommy Joe gave Bob Long the remaining $5,000 and Bob was on his way to becoming a full-fledged franchisee of Pizza Hut. Or was he? As fate would have it, a tornado hit Tommy Joe's Texas ranch. Tommy called and asked, "Have you cashed the check yet?" "No! Not yet!" "Well, don't. I need it for repairs on the ranch." Swish, there went the money… gone with the wind!!!

Bob Long, not to be defeated, decided his best bet now was his Packer roommate, Bob Skoronski. (Green Bay Packers 1956-1968) Skoronski was a Captain of the team and a good business man. Bob Long started his sales pitch on Skoronski and he told him about this great opportunity, and about the wonderful pizza that Pizza Hut served. Skoronski then inquired if the pizza was like the pizza they serve in <u>his home state</u> of Connecticut. Sighing, Bob asked, "What is <u>Connecticut</u> pizza like?" "Well, it is really thick and is covered with all sorts of toppings." "Hmmm! Okay, I think they can do that!" So, he called the Pizza Hut home office and asked where the nearest Pizza Hut was to Green Bay and was told it was in Des Moines, IA. (*Ha*!) I don't know if you have ever traveled from Green Bay to Des Moines by automobile, but if you haven't, don't even think about it. You can't get <u>there</u> from <u>there</u>!

Bob Long phoned ahead, explaining to the Des Moines

Pizza Hut he was coming, and bringing a prospective investor. Would they, **please,** load the pizza up with lots and lots of toppings? They did exactly as they were told. "This pizza is **terrible**!" cried Skoronski. "There is so much topping you can't find the crust." Needless to say, Bob Skoronski, much to his chagrin, did not invest in Pizza Hut with the young entrepreneur.

By now Long was really dejected, so one afternoon he stopped at the Left Guard in Appleton, where Fuzzy, Max, and some others were gambling at the bar, and he told them what had happened. Fuzzy Thurston, displaying his "great-heart," said he would take a piece of the remaining amount needed to close the deal. Fuzzy told Max to do the same! Max hemmed and hawed, and finally Fuzzy said, "Max, you lose that much every day playing Gin Rummy. Take the action!" At last, Max did… and so did an attorney who was visiting from Madison. Three of them split the $5000. FINALLY!!! Bob Long had his Pizza Hut franchise.

Through the years Long made extra sure Max McGee

received the annual stock reports, and he sent him <u>extra</u> information concerning the progress of Pizza Hut. According to Bob, Max never seemed to pay much attention, and eventually, the Pepsi Corporation bought out Pizza Hut.

Max operated one of the restaurants in the Left Guard chain in Bloomington, MN called Maximillian's. It was going under and he wanted to convert it into a Mexican Restaurant. The businessman with whom Max was going into business has a wife named ChiChi. Max called Bob Long and asked him what the Pizza Hut stock was now worth, saying he needed some capital to invest in ChiChi's. Bob said the original $1,666.66, which Max had begrudgingly invested long ago, was <u>now</u> worth about $265,000. Max used this money to parley himself in the ChiChi's restaurant venture. I am told ChiChi's stock went from 11cents per share to $14, in a short time. Subsequently, Max McGee became a millionaire… and so did Bob Long!

One could fill a book with stories about Max McGee. He should write a book about his life… and so should Paul. Perhaps they will and it will certainly be entertaining. I especially like <u>Paul</u>'s take… on his own life. He is <u>lighthearted</u> about the way his life unfolded, and about the grand lifestyle his football career has afforded him. Paul, teasingly, says he asked his wife to put the following epitaph on his tombstone:

HERE LIES

PAUL HORNUNG

Football Player

Who went through life on a <u>scholarship</u>

~~~

My husband was a dentist, and he always teased that his tombstone should read:

HERE LIES

MATTHEW SULLIVAN

Dentist

Filling his last cavity

But that's another story!

A hung-over Max McGee gives #22 Kansas City Chiefs', Willie Mitchell, a free ride at Super Bowl I. From the Collection of Vernon Biever (copyright)

Boyd Dowler concentrates on his <u>only</u> mission... catching and holding on to the ball.

(MI2) MILWUAKEE, AUG. 23 -- PRAISE FROM THE TOP --
Flanker Bob Long, #80, of Green Bay Packers is congratulated by coach
Vince Lombardi and Doug Hart, #43, after his 80-yard touchdown run in the
fourth quarter against the Chicago Bears at County Stadium Saturday. Long
scored on a pass from Zeke Bratowski. The Packers defeated the Bears in
the Shrine game, 31-14. (AP WIREPHOTO) (CK72030ck stf) 1965.

LONG'S LOVE STORY

When you meet Bob Long, he will usually tell you of one of the funnier things which happened to him… when he was young and single. First of all, ladies, Bob Long is a 6'3" and 203 lbs… he is a tall, good-looking hunk… a real doll! The rest of his teammates knew that, too! It seems because he was so good-looking and eligible, one of his teammates was using his identity to pick up girls. (Bob says I cannot tell you who it is, even though I know. It took me four years to get him to divulge the identity. But, I am susceptible to bribery!)

Bob was alone one evening at the Left End Restaurant in Manitowoc, WI. He noticed a very, good-looking, young lady, at the other end of the bar.

It was after the 1966 Super Bowl, he was wearing his diamond Super Bowl ring, and he flashed it so the girl would notice him. He sent a drink down to her and then, walked down to introduce himself. "Hello, I'm Bob Long. How are you?" She looked up at him and said with surprise, "You're not Bob Long!" Bob said, "Sure I am." "Come on, no you're not." "I certainly am," protested Bob. "I'll show you my driver's license to prove it." The young lady insisted, "I know you are not Bob Long because I met Bob Long right here, last night, and you are not '**the Bob Long**' I met last night!" Much to the young lady's dismay she finally realized she had been duped, and he realized someone was using his bachelor status to attract young ladies. When he was at practice the next morning he told the story to the team and when one of the teammates responded with a wee bit of guilt and hardy laughter, he knew who it was. Besides, the young lady had described this interloper in detail which also confirmed Bob's suspicion.

When I told Bob Long I was writing this book, he said I would probably sell many copies to my fellow Green Bay Packer fans, but voiced concern that the Lombardi Packers would not be pleased. Let me be clear! This book is not an embarrassing tell-all so I had to disagree with Bob, reasoning that all this happened 40+ years ago and if some are offended, they need to get over it. Ron Kramer agrees, saying there is nothing I could tell which would hurt anyone's life now. Paul Hornung says members of the team are public figures, and if they don't want the <u>truth</u> to be written about them, they had best do <u>nothing</u> to discredit themselves. If naughty…one must pay the piper! Of course, I do <u>not</u> want to hurt anyone by the stories I tell in this book. I do feel however, if I don't tell them, no one will. They are too special and precious to lose, and I am sure most of my readers will agree. Also, by their own admission, many of my football player friends tell me they have not read a book in years. It is understood… if <u>they</u> want to know what I've written about them, they will have to <u>read</u> the book. Consider this book my personal contribution to the literacy of some of the former Green Bay Packers!

It should be known… women are not the only ones who have football heroes. Sometimes, football heroes have football heroes, and Bob Long is one of them. Bob's football hero is Boyd Dowler, and he often refers to Boyd as "my hero." Lombardi called Boyd Dowler, "Mr. Clean," but those of us who know Boyd believe he had Lombardi fooled. Don't misunderstand me… Boyd is a "good guy," but he had a lot of <u>fun</u> which Lombardi knew nothing about. He sort of pulled the wool over the "old man's eyes," if you know what I mean. And, ladies, he is very good-looking! There are <u>few</u> women who would not swoon if Boyd Dowler flashed his "baby blues." But forget it! He's been happily married to his high school sweetheart for about a thousand years, or at least, it <u>seems</u> that long!

Boyd is a <u>true</u> <u>friend</u> to his teammates… extremely loyal and concerned about their well-being. As with all members of the Lombardi team, they "flat-out" **love** each other. They <u>always have</u>… and they <u>always will</u>! Today when they meet, they usually embrace one another. When they part, they hug and sometimes kiss each other. I am sure this is because of what they accomplished <u>together,</u> and because of the memories they share. They played football with <u>love</u> for each other and the game. Fuzzy says, **<u>"I love you,"</u>** to them. He says, "…we don't know if we will ever meet again." We all need to heed this lesson and tell our loved ones how much they mean to us. To better understand this, all you have to see is the new stadium in Green Bay to realize what the <u>love</u> of these men helped create. If you have not seen Lambeau Field, <u>you need to go and see it</u>. It is awe-inspiring and it stands as a fitting memorial to all the <u>great</u> <u>spirits</u> who have passed through its gates and given their hearts to the Green Bay Packers. <u>It must have been</u>… **love**!

Come to think of it, Fuzzy was and is, <u>notorious</u> for openly showing his affection to his teammates. When Dan Currie was traded to the L.A. Rams for Carroll Dale, everybody missed Dan, especially Fuzzy. Fuzzy loves Dan and Dan loves Fuzzy! When the Packers kicked off against the Rams in the Los Angeles Coliseum in the fall of 1965, Fuzzy arranged to be on the field for the kick-off. He knew Dan would be on special teams for the Rams and on the kick-off, Fuzzy raced down the field and tackled Dan. Jumping on top of him, he tore off Dan's helmet, and smothered him with kisses in front of thousands of people. "Get off me, Fuzzy, what are you doing?" giggled Dan. See! I told you <u>these</u> are **love stories!**

And it must have been **love** when Boyd Dowler took the rookie, Bob Long, under his wing. Boyd affectionately nicknamed him "BULLET," after Bullet Bob Hayes, the Dallas Cowboy's end, who was <u>supposed</u> to be one of the fastest men alive. Bob says every time Boyd Dowler called him "BULLET," his (Bob's) chest would swell, and he could actually envision himself being faster than Hayes. Remember friends, we become what we think about most of the time. So, Boyd prompted the rookie from Kansas into making some <u>fast</u> moves. Years later, when Boyd was a coach under George Allen in the L.A Rams organization, he needed a wide receiver and he called on Bob Long to help him. Bob was just getting his business ventures underway and was moving away from football. "Hey, Bullet," beckoned Boyd, "the Rams need you." "No way!" he said. "I'm too busy… doing <u>other</u> things." "But Bullet… **I** <u>need you!</u>" How could he refuse his <u>football</u> <u>hero</u>? He signed on to play for Boyd Dowler and the Rams, and did a great job. That's **love**, baby!!!

GUILT BY ASSOCIATION

My association with Paul Hornung and other Packer players sometimes caused problems for me. Early in the 1960's, I went to modeling school in Milwaukee and became a professional model. There is an internationally-known, high-fashion model named "Twiggy," and she is as thin as a rail, so other models in those days judged themselves by <u>her</u> measurements. I was <u>not</u> skinny! (*Not by a long shot*!) SO…people in the modeling business referred to me as the <u>wholesome-type</u>. Yah, you betcha! Like… Wisconsin butter and cheese! My saving grace was having a good personality and being friendly to people… and I was attractive. As a result, I was asked to work at Sport Shows and Home Shows, and I did some lunch-time modeling for various department stores. I modeled clothing; walking around, talking to the people while they ate lunch. I was well received in places where friendliness and conversations with the public were required. I was very good at that!

For me, modeling is <u>not</u> all it is cracked up to be! I had several run-ins with men who hired models for the express purpose of forcing themselves upon them. One particular man in the carpet business was a real lecher! He told me he had heard that I was a girlfriend of Paul Hornung, so he was <u>sure</u> I was giving it out. He hired two of us (models) to demonstrate carpet at the Home Show at McCormick Place in Chicago. He decided he was <u>not</u> going to bring us home if we didn't have sex with him. (*Man, I wish this was happening today! I would <u>own</u> his house and business!*) In those days, women did not have the laws to <u>protect</u> them like we do now. On this particular trip to Chicago, the other girl and I got the man drunk in order to save ourselves. He had taken us out to dinner at the Camellia Room in the Drake Hotel, and Helen Morgan was the entertainer who had a popular hit song called "<u>Fascination</u>." Perhaps you've heard it on the "<u>oldies</u>" radio stations. Anyhow, with our help, this little varmint passed out right in the middle of her show. Miss Morgan seemed to intuitively grasp the situation as she stood over him, with microphone in hand, and sang "Fascination" directly to the back of his head (which was buried in his plate of food), and she delighted the audience. The next day he was really upset with us and this is when he threatened, saying he would not pay us for the time we had worked for him. He said we had to sleep with him in order to get paid. In other words…no <u>sex</u> - no <u>money</u>$!!! Unfortunately, we didn't have enough money to leave and get back to Milwaukee. In those days you needed C-A-S-H. That is <u>still</u> the <u>only</u> way to spell relief! **<u>C</u>-<u>A</u>-<u>S</u>-<u>H</u>**! There was no such thing as a credit card then. He had planned the entire excursion so we would be totally at his mercy, and without cash. My friend, the other model, borrowed money from a bell-hop, which he gladly provided once he heard about our situation. With his pocket-change she was able to make a call from a phone booth to her boyfriend while I kept the "creep" occupied. The boyfriend drove to Chicago (90 miles) to pick us up. We thought the hours during which we awaited his arrival, would never end. It was an unpleasant experience, but it was also a terrific lesson about the real world. (*You are no longer in Kansas, Toto.*) I vowed

<u>never</u> to be caught in a bind like this again; without money or transportation. A woman should always take enough <u>cash</u> to get out of bad or uncomfortable circumstances. I found that this type of <u>uncomfortable</u> situation occurred frequently in the modeling racket.

(You little bastard, I hope you're still alive to read this… this is my <u>revenge</u> on you!)

At about the same time, there was a group of models in Milwaukee who decided they wanted to give respectability to the modeling profession. Apparently this group had experienced some of the same things I had experienced in Chicago. They wanted respect from the community, so they formed a "club" with a fancy name so everyone would think we (models) were <u>high</u> class. Some of my girlfriends were already members, and they encouraged me to try for acceptance into this exclusive group. They said it would help my career and I agreed, but privately and personally, I sort of felt like we were the "<u>MEAT</u>" in the "meat and potatoes" modeling industry. I agreed to go to the gathering and enter my name on the recruiting list. What an experience! The meeting was held at the residence of a relative of Buckets Goldenberg; convening on a beautiful Sunday afternoon, in the living room of a lovely apartment. There were 4 or 5 of us applying for membership, and my girlfriends were convinced I would be a "shoe-in." All entries had to get up and talk about their main accomplishments in modeling. I was fresh from the bad experience in Chicago, but I didn't mention my escape as an accomplishment, although I thought it was. I told them about my career plans for modeling jobs in the future, and they all seemed pleased with me. Finally, it was time to cast the votes.

Perhaps my affiliation with Paul Hornung, or my friendship with Buckets Goldenburg, had preceded me to the meeting that Sunday afternoon. I will never know for sure… but why should it have made a difference? I hadn't the foggiest idea that Buckets was visiting with some of his relatives in the next room that day. Just as the group had marked their secret ballots and was about to hand them in, Buckets opened the door of a side room, and started to exit through the living room in which we were sitting. When he saw me and I saw him, I stood up and went to greet him. We embraced and pecked each other's cheek, like a father and daughter. Then he left, expressing a very courteous "Good Afternoon!" to the rest of the ladies. Turning around to sit down again, I saw the ladies reaching for their ballots so they could change their vote. I almost started to cry because I knew what was happening! All of the applicants were inducted into the group… except me. Some of the model-members seemed embarrassed… as they had been blatantly, obvious. I thought they were cruel. (*I am getting further and further from Kansas, Toto.*)

Of course I felt badly and shed some tears, but I didn't cry for long. That day I learned a great lesson about rushing to quick judgment of people. It is unfair and very hurtful! Don't let it happen! Seek the truth, but do <u>not</u> pass judgment. When I called home and told my father, he laughed and said I didn't want to belong to that "phony, old bunch," anyhow… a typical father's reaction! Initially, when I told Buckets, he was flattered to think they thought I was his "Sweetie" and he was my "Sugar Daddy." However, the longer he thought about how ridiculous it was, the angrier he became. Buckets was a Ukrainian-Jew, born in the Ukraine… he was a very, proper man and detested being judged in such a way. He and his family had suffered other indignities… this was an indignity for him… and he didn't like it. He expressed his displeasure to one of the modeling agencies, and to the female relative in whose apartment we had the meeting. For a long time after, he discontinued the modeling at Pappy's restaurant at lunchtime. Of course, I somewhat became an anathema in the Milwaukee modeling industry and I lost my desire to model. (*OH…Dorothy, it was all in your imagination!*) I'm not sure if it was my imagination or not, but regardless, I had a bad taste in my mouth about modeling, and soon after, I moved to Chicago. I got completely out of **Dodge**! (*That's in Kansas, too, ya' know!*)

In those days I was young, single, and even if I do say so myself, a rather pretty girl. My mother and father are both good-looking… and my looks are a <u>gift</u> for which I have always been grateful. At the time, I could turn a head easily and often did. Several fellows asked for dates, and I was somewhat <u>sure of myself</u> around men, perhaps because of my relationships with some well-known, football players in Green Bay. I <u>like</u> being around men… I understand them… and they sometimes like being around me. My father raised me to be a man's woman. All things considered, men are more fun than women, and are not as judgmental… as women can sometimes be. Sorry, ladies, but it's the truth. (*Not that I do not love and cherish my females friends. I do, but they are few in number*) Athletes were my primary interest because they were fun and exciting. I was bored with other fellows, and as I recall, I was not truly interested in anyone who didn't play football. Because of this, I learned a valuable lesson about men. Some American men can become jealous, intimidated, and unsure of themselves when they think they are competing with a professional athlete. I believe it was Coco Channel who said, if you understand that most men behave like children, you will have an easier time accepting them and their actions. I am not so sure if Coco is right… I believe the real truth is… some men don't grow up to learn who they are. They have never taken the time to look themselves in the mirror, eyeball-to-eyeball, and say, "Hello, who are **you**? Let's get to **know** each other… what kind of person do you want to become?" Unfortunately, some American men are required to grow up while being forced to fit into many roles, and haven't a clue about their **true** identity. Terry

Bradshaw discovered what I mean and in his book, "**Keep It Simple,**" and he has a sentence in the dedication which says it all… "I was forced to come face-to-face with my own face." (Bradshaw 2002) (*Good for you, Terry*!)

Sometimes I notice insecurity in men but I don't discount them, because I think sooner or later, they will figure themselves out. I hope it's <u>sooner</u>, rather than later. To further explain what I mean… when I've <u>shared</u> this book with some male acquaintances they back off, unwilling to comment on the book or its content. I ask them to <u>critically</u> comment because I will <u>respect</u> their opinion. Their <u>silence</u> is profound, and it tells me they haven't personally, <u>faced</u> their <u>own face</u>. They cannot give me their opinion because they do <u>not</u> have one. Maybe their parents didn't teach them to get to know themselves. Something is missing! Maybe the parents do not personally <u>know</u> <u>themselves</u>, either. Perhaps no one ever taught <u>them</u> that it is <u>important</u> to "<u>Know Thyself</u>." As a result, we have a bunch of people running around who don't know <u>who they are</u>, <u>what they are</u>, or <u>why they're here</u>. There is <u>little</u> soul-searching going on. As a result, some of us must tolerate a bunch of wishy-washy, non-descript, "wandering generalities" who insist on getting in the way of those who want to lead directed and goal-oriented lives. No wonder the world is screwed up! Only those who are truly **sure** of themselves stand for something, and these men have positive, constructive criticism which is helpful to me. Interestingly, I have found this book <u>can</u> be used like a meter for figuring out men's maturity, self-confidence and self-image… and to my sorrow, I have discovered some "chest-less" men. The book was not intended to expose these results and the discovery has been disappointing for me, but I find some men don't know how to react or what to say. When the book is out I am sure I will receive an abundance of comments, ranging from compliments… to insults, and many, because of personal insecurities, will be inaccurate and/or insincere. I think this is because men <u>allow</u> themselves to feel <u>inferior</u> in some way when it comes to comparing themselves with athletes. Probably wanting to become a professional athlete themselves, they found out that they didn't have <u>what it takes</u>. (*"Snap out of it!" said Cher.*) Everyone can't be everything… but you <u>can</u> be the <u>best</u> of who <u>you</u> are. (*So, for goodness sake…figure out what and who your are! And…hurry up, will ya, please!*) In their defense, men are no different from women who become intimidated by a superbly, foxy-looking female with big breasts, who the guys find attractive and make a big fuss over. (*Been there, done that!*)

The husband of a girlfriend commented saying I was probably going to, also, expose his wife's love-life before they had married. I was surprised to know he is still intimidated about nothing that never happened 40 years ago, except in his mind. Perhaps he secretly thinks his lovely wife would rather have been with Paul Hornung than with him. (*Sad!*) Besides, his wife never looked sideways at anyone, except her husband. Lots of distress can be born of imaginings!

In the early 1960's, I was young, naïve, and looking back now, I would have to say, really dumb. I could have had my pick of some very nice fellows… but marrying, settling down with a pillar of the community, living in suburbia, and raising children, was not yet on my "Wish List." I was not interested in a fine, stable, young man who would be faithful, put me in a white house with a picket fence… give me lots of kids, and relegate me to the "boon docks." If I had had common sense, this is exactly what I should have been looking for. Isn't this what all normal young women want? Well, I wasn't normal, that's for sure. But down deep, I probably wanted it, too … but not just yet. I am sure if this had happened to me, I would not have been there for very long. At that time in my life it would have been too dull… so… I bought a little plaque at my Church which reads, "Lord, make me virtuous… but not yet!" I still have it!

Grace L., the girlfriend who dated Max McGee, fell for a fine young man in Milwaukee named Bill. Bill owned his own company and was indeed, a pillar of the community… and he was crazy about Grace. He had a roommate named John, who would double-date with them sometimes. One evening I was invited to go out with the three of them, and I discovered Grace and Bill were trying to fix me up with John. By reputation, John was a "ladies man" and by all standards, a "great catch." I didn't care if he was or was not! Apparently he thought that when I met him, I would fall all over him as other women had. I went to dinner but, when he asked me out again, I refused.

I wasn't playing hard to get… I simply was not interested.
Well… it is hard to totally describe the reaction I got from John.
Because I refused him, and was <u>not</u> attracted to him… he went
"nuts" over me, IMMEDIATELY! He hardly even knew me.
All he knew was… I was someone… he couldn't get. He called,
sent roses, and wrote letters inviting me to lovely functions.
He even bought me an expensive dog because I had expressed
an interest in the breed, and he named the dog "Cointreau,"
because he heard I liked this particular After-Dinner liqueur
called Cointreau. I received all this attention just because I had
said "No." It blew my mind! Why couldn't I be this way with
Paul Hornung? Perhaps then, he would become crazy about me,
too! But, I figured out it would be impossible to do this with
Paul because Paul didn't stay in one place long enough to make
the plan work. I was learning about men… so this is what they
mean by "playing <u>hard-to-get</u>." But I wasn't! I did not know
for sure what I had done to cause this type of reaction. All I had
done was show <u>disinterest</u> and refuse a date.

After much coaxing, I finally agreed to join all of them for
dinner. My Lord… talk about being the <u>center</u> of attention. John

became overly-indulgent, and of course, I was flattered by his adulation. He asked me to come home and meet his family, so I went for a weekend to a lovely family home in Southern Wisconsin, where I met his mother and the uncle-patriarch of the family, who happened to be the president of a major railroad.

About a month later, after dating often, but without <u>any</u> commitment, John said he was going to take a trip to Florida. He said he would be gone for about a week. As you recall... I was living with Grace L. and Bill was at our apartment almost all of the time. I know he was not spying on me, but he could not help but observe my comings and goings. One day Paul Hornung called, said he was coming to Milwaukee for the weekend, and asked if I would be available... for a date. Naturally I said, "YES!" I loved dating Paul... I went... and had a great time.

When the week was up... I didn't get a call from John who I thought was crazy about me. More time passed, and I began to think that John had not returned. Bill assured me that indeed, he had returned. Then I inquired about his health and/or if something unfortunate had happened to him. "<u>No</u>, <u>nothing</u>!" I did not try to contact <u>him</u> and I really didn't care if I saw him again, or not! But…I was curious as to what had happened. Then one evening John called and stated, in a rather abrupt and belligerent tone… if I wanted to know what had turned him **off**, he would tell me. Like a fool, I asked for the reason! He said he <u>knew</u> I had gone out on a date with Paul Hornung while he was away. I said, "So what?" (*Was I being tested?*) …and then he said something like… he was not going to tolerate a woman who would do such a socially, unacceptable thing. (*Oh… gimme' a break*!) I got the message! John thought <u>nice</u> girls didn't run around with professional football players! But was that <u>really</u> the reason? I don't think so! I think he was insecure and felt he <u>could</u> not and/or did not want to compete with Paul Hornung. Henry Ford said, "… If you think you <u>can</u>… you <u>can</u>. If you think you <u>can't</u>… you <u>can't</u>. Either way, <u>you're right</u>!" Well, Buster, you're right! You <u>can't</u>… don't let the door hit you in the butt! Thanks, Paul, <u>you</u> saved me from a life of boring mediocrity! See? You really <u>are</u> my HERO!

THE KING'S X

When Texas children play hide and seek… <u>home</u> <u>free</u>, or the place of safety, is called "<u>The King's X</u>." When we play this game in Wisconsin, we pick a tree or a particular place and call out, "olly, olly, oxen, all in <u>free</u>." They both mean the same thing… in Texas or Wisconsin. "The King's X" is a <u>safe</u> place where no one can <u>get</u> you… or <u>bother</u> you. What a great name for a saloon and restaurant!

In the early 1960's Green Bay had a <u>King's X</u> and it was a place where we felt safe and could have fun, just like children. We were <u>child**like**</u>, and sometimes, we were child**ish**! The King's X was a bar and restaurant started by a couple of Texas cousins named Whittenton. These cousins also ran a country club in El Paso, TX and Jesse Whittenton (Green Bay Packers 1958-1964) and his cousin, Don, are the visionaries who sponsored their Golf Pro, Lee Trevino, in the PGA Circuit.

When they came to Green Bay they brought the whole family with them… and knowing this family was delightful. First of all, there was the patriarch, Urshell, who must have been in his 60's during these years, but was always looking to meet a young lady to squire around. He referred to these young ladies as "debutantes." What a handsome man! When I finally got to see Jesse again, after 35 years, he had come to look just like his father… as ever, very handsome!

Don and his wife, Claudia, were the proprietors of the bar and restaurant. Claudia was great to me and was the epitome of what I thought a Southwestern lady should be… <u>solid</u>! She did her part to keep the business running smoothly while caring for her children. Her husband, Don, and cousin, Jesse, worked too, and I think <u>they</u> had <u>most</u> of the fun. Jesse was paid a great deal of attention by the ladies because Jesse was one, really good-looking dude. He has a great build and he talks with an <u>El Paso</u>

accent, whatever that is… <u>Texan</u>, I guess. Jesse played for the Green Bay Packers as a defensive back and he was really good. To add to all this wonderment, Jesse Whittenton loves women, and he believes in marrying the women he loves. So much so, that at this writing, he has been married seven times…twice to his first wife.

It was so much fun to go to the King's X! I would party in Milwaukee, and then get lonesome for the place, take off at midnight, drive up Highway 41, and try to get to the King's X before they had "Last Call." I usually made it, but I shudder when I think of it now, and of the chances I took to get there. I think I was really WILD! About a year ago my teenage daughter called me on a Sunday evening in December and said, "Hi, Mom! Guess <u>where I am</u>?… "I'm in Green Bay." Oh, my Lord… I thought my stomach was going to drop out of me. "I just drove up from Madison to see what's happening here. I thought maybe I could get into the Packer game, but there are no tickets."

Now, I don't know what made me so nervous about this,

except for the fact I <u>never</u> called my mother when I was in Green Bay. I certainly did **<u>NOT</u>** want her to know where I was. When I went to Green Bay I was up to <u>no-good,</u> but my daughter is quite the opposite from me. That evening I spoke calmly to her and said, "Have fun, Honey! Don't stay <u>too</u> late, and be careful driving home." Then I prayed <u>all</u> night. She called the next day saying she had stopped in at Fuzzy Thurston's bar, but didn't know anyone except Fuzzy, and he was busy talking with other people. She said she didn't hang around, as I would have done years ago, looking for action… and she had driven back to the University in Madison early in the evening. (*Whew!*)

There were many times when I went to Green Bay and did not have a <u>good</u> time. Either, things had not worked out with seeing Paul, or the team didn't win, and so on. I remember one time my father called me and inquired about my weekend. He was always very leery about my association with the players, probably because he was a man himself, and surmised what was going on, and of course, he never blamed <u>me</u> for what was happening. I was crying when he called and he told me to "quit blubbering" over men such as these. He told me that I was far superior in intelligence, character, breeding, and that I out-classed them. Then he said something which I will never forget, and I am still grateful to my dad for saying it. He said, "Just remember, Sandy, I wouldn't trade <u>one</u> of your little fingers for the whole damn league." (*SO THERE*!) He certainly gave me a supportive statement to assure me of his love and my own self-worth. Just before she died, my Mom and I were driving somewhere, and she said, "You know, Sandy, looking back, you were doing so well <u>until</u> you met those football players!" Hmm! Her words are food for thought…and I <u>have </u>thought about them a lot! Was my mother <u>right</u>? Were football players my downfall? Could be! Football players have certainly had an effect on my life, both good and bad, and I am sure many people would tell me it is **not** the best effect I might have gotten, had I associated with a <u>different</u> group of people. (*OH, WELL*! *It's a little late to worry about that!*) I rationalize my fascination with them by the fact that I am a fairly, big girl, and my dad always teased me about finding a large man, who was strong enough to carry me over the threshold. The football player's size was my best hope of that becoming a reality.

Back to the King's X-

At the time, Jesse was between wives. I think this is true, but it was hard to keep track… the marriages were frequent. One night Jesse introduced me to TEX-MEX food! I will never forget him… laughing, popping a **hot,** Mexican, chili pepper into my mouth while we raided the refrigerators in the King's X kitchen after hours. I swear… my hair stood on end. My eyes watered so badly the mascara ran down my cheeks. Jesse thought it was hilarious, and I probably would have, too, if it had been happening to someone else. (*Very funny, Jess*!)

On Monday nights the King's X served an old-fashioned sauerkraut and spare-ribs dinner. Most of the players, usually with wives or girlfriends, would come to indulge. It was fun… like a family-gathering with everyone getting together for a hot (almost-like-home-cooked) meal. I recall Paul and Herb Adderley (G.B. 1961-69) loved to come and enjoy this delicious feast. One particular couple, Olive and Henry Jordan, usually showed up, too. Talk about a <u>honey</u>… I wish everyone could meet Olive Jordan. She is so together and sure of herself... exuding an air of confidence. At dinner, she laughed and joked...taking the time to come around and say "Hello" to everyone. Usually, Henry was right behind her, agreeing with her enthusiasm. It did not matter whether Olive knew someone, or not... she was like a hostess going around making everyone feel welcome. I have always thought it was because she and Henry had such a good marriage. Both of them were <u>always</u> happy and smiling... had excellent, outgoing personalities, and made everyone else feel good. In the bar scene, Henry never drank anything but tea, and it was fun to hear Olive tell about partying, and Henry, in the morning, feeling worse than anyone else because he had imbibed in too much **tea** the night before. Whenever there was a need for a player spokesperson, Henry was the one usually chosen by his teammates to be the speaker or master of ceremonies. He was the MC for Bart Starr Day when President Nixon came to Green Bay to honor Bart. Sadly, Henry died at the age of 42 years! After playing football for ten years at Green Bay, he became the General Manager of the Summerfest in Milwaukee. I thought this was a perfect fit of job and person. He had everything it would take to make

Summerfest a great success. Now, as I understand it, the job was extremely stressful, and one day while Henry was working-out at the Milwaukee Athletic Club, he died of a massive heart attack. I lived in Washington D. C. at the time, remember hearing the news, and crying my eyes out. What a terrible loss of a really, <u>super</u> fellow! I am sure my friends of the Packers felt far worse. I sat down and wrote a 4 or 5 page letter to Olive, recalling the fun times in which Henry took part. She wrote back thanking me profusely for remembering! What a doll! I felt so badly for her.

Jesse used the front apartment above the King's X, as his home away from home. There is no telling who or what might be found if one ventured upstairs to this <u>pad</u>. It was a stopping-off place for many of the players, and you may call it a "den of iniquity" if you like… because you would be correct. In this day and age, it would most likely be considered <u>off-limits</u>. After hours everyone who had a "welcome" would end-up in Jesse's apartment and some people who were not welcome… were always trying to get in. There was booze available and sometimes there was a poker or gin game going on. I know on occasion there was a <u>strip</u>-poker game, which I somehow always managed to avoid. Believe it or not, I was pretty shy with events of this type... I did not think I had a very good body... and I certainly did not want a bunch of strangers to see it. The party which began downstairs at the bar, inevitably ended up... upstairs. We would party until everyone fell asleep wherever they landed. One of my girlfriends woke up one morning in a closet, and couldn't remember how she got there. She thinks she was trying to hide from an unwelcome fellow who was in hot pursuit of her.

One did <u>not</u> get to sleep <u>late</u> in Jesse's apartment because at 5 A.M., the <u>pickle</u> factory across the street <u>jolted</u> into operation, waking everyone. If we had been partying in New York City with the New York Giants, we would most likely have been awakened by the sounds of early-morning Manhattan traffic. But since we disliked the N.Y. Giants and were in Green Bay, <u>dawn</u> was announced by noise from a <u>pickle</u> factory. (*Be satisfied!... You were <u>there</u>, for goodness sake!*) But there <u>is</u> a difference between New York and Green Bay! (*Duh!*) A BIG difference! In the morning most everyone would leave for a

<u>quieter</u> place, where we could <u>recover</u> from hangovers and have a good breakfast. For the <u>privileged</u> among us that was sometimes downstairs in the kitchen of the King's X.

There was a very, nice man named Pat Martin who was a private pilot and a Green Bay businessman. He was Paul Hornung's buddy and was <u>like</u> Paul's <u>personal</u> pilot… he flew Paul wherever he wanted to go. When Paul was drafted into the U.S. Army (1961) and stationed at Fort Riley, Kansas, Pat Martin was the one who flew him back and forth so he could play all the games... compliments of Uncle Sam and the President of the United States, John F. Kennedy. Coach Lombardi called President Kennedy and asked if he would make an allowance for Paul to play football on Sundays and the President told Lombardi he would allow it, saying the Viet Nam war could not be won in a day, like a football game. Nothing like pulling a few strings! See what happens if one knows the right people.

Early one morning, as Paul and I were (sleeping) in the front bedroom of Jesse's apartment, Pat Martin came bounding through the door. "Paul! Paul! Come on, get up! Get up! Pauly, wake up! I've been <u>looking</u> for <u>you</u> all over town. Come on! Wake up… we have to go! (pause) …Oh… Hiya, Sandy!" "Hello, Pat!" I said, and with that Paul gave me a little peck on the cheek, said he'd call, and was **gone**! Lordy! Lordy! How I hated Pat Martin! He was always getting Paul to fly away!

I recall one evening very late, maybe 3 or 4 A.M…. I was going to leave the party at Jesse's apartment <u>early</u>!!! (*Why?*) I have no idea why! (*Me…leave early?*) I started down the hall to the back stairway (the only way to get in and out), and was stopped dead in my tracks at the top of the steps by a pile of people. There were three of them, all lying on their backs facing the ceiling, and they were passed out <u>cold</u>. I went back into the apartment to get Jesse, and he turned on the hall lights to better assess the situation. When we could see better, we realized there were two, really large Native American men <u>lying</u> side by side, facing up, blocking the stairs. It looked as though they had <u>lain</u> down and made a bed. (*I am a teacher…I should know better than to try and explain whether there were "laying or lying." Oh, who gives a darn…! You get the picture.*) Lying in the middle, on top of them, was a very large Native American woman also facing up. We didn't know what to do, but, we hollered at them, we nudged them, and someone exploded a cherry bomb for noise! No response! Jesse went in and filled a pail with <u>ice</u> <u>cold</u> water. Standing back toward the middle of the hallway, he bowled the water at the trio. We expected them to wake with a start, but there was NO RESPONSE! We tried everything imaginable to get down the stairs, even crawling over them, but their feet were resting on the top step, and their bodies filled the passageway. The stairwell was steep and dangerous and it was impossible. By this time there was a small crowd of other people gathering who wanted to leave as well, but could not. Finally we gave up, and everyone went back into Jesse's apartment and partied some more. When the pickle factory started up at 5 A.M., we looked out the door and down the hall…and the trio was gone. ONLY IN GREEN BAY!

One time I went to the apartment during the daytime, because I had left my coat there, and wanted to retrieve it. When I walked in, the place was void of people, but I knew Dapper Dan Currie had been there the night before, and had gone from there to practice. How did I know? I knew because Dan is a meticulous dresser, usually with a shirt and tie. He had obviously left his shirt, along with the tie, at the apartment and had most likely gone to practice in a borrowed casual shirt. Someone had carefully fitted his dress-shirt over the back of a straight-backed kitchen chair, had buttoned it up, and had carefully tied the tie. It was comical to see!

One of Jesse's faithful bartenders, "Boots" Baker, bought the King's X from the Whittentons and operated it until the middle 1990's. Though Boots did a great job, once Jesse was gone, for me it was <u>never</u> the same. I always, selfishly, believe that Jesse retired too soon. (*Is that selfish?*) It used to break my heart going back to the King's X, remembering all the laughter and the great times we had there… <u>all of us</u> together. Can you ever get <u>enough</u> of a <u>good thing</u>? **<u>NEVER</u>**! Dear readers, may you <u>always</u> have a **<u>King's X</u>** in your life!

KING'S X
Just for you!

HENRY JORDAN, DEFENSIVE TACKLE, GREEN BAY PACKERS

Henry Jordan died in Milwaukee in 1977. He was inducted into the
Professional Football-Hall of Fame in 1995.
(Green Bay Packers 1959-1969)

MY FIRST CHAMPIONSHIP

Green Bay Packer fans remember <u>every</u> play of a championship game. Many remember <u>every</u> detail of <u>every</u> game, championship or not. Remembering like this occurs when one is focused. An example of this happening is when John F. Kennedy was assassinated. Those of us who were around remember our <u>exact</u> location when we heard the news… we were focused. This phenomenon is sometimes called "a defining moment." Packer fans have <u>many</u> defining moments, because they are passionately focused on <u>everything</u> which involves the Green Bay Packers.

I was focused when the Green Bay Packers won the Championship game on Sunday, December 31, 1961… I was there. It was New Year's Eve, and my roommate, Grace L., could <u>not</u> go… because she had to work at the Grand Opening of the Swan Theatre in Milwaukee. However, her boyfriend, Bill, was going to Green Bay for the game and festivities. I asked if I could ride with him and he said, "Sure." He'd been invited to stay at the home of friends and said I was welcome to stay there, also. I had no intentions of staying at a private home in Green Bay on this particular weekend. In fact, I had no intention of <u>sleeping</u>! I went along for the ride, and enjoyed a great party at Bill's friend's house on Saturday night before the game. The party was wild! The host got himself very drunk, very early in the evening. His new bride put him to bed several times. I recall he was so <u>excited</u> about the Packer events, he continued to sober up over and over, and party again and again. At the end of the evening, whenever that was, he went to bed with a Vienna sausage in his mouth, and woke up with it in his mouth the next morning! UGH! Gross!

Bill was a <u>name</u>-<u>dropper</u> and through conversations with him, some people at the party learned I was friends with many Packer players. They asked personal questions and wanted to know if I would be seeing anyone <u>special</u> over the weekend… namely, Paul Hornung. I knew the answer to that question depended greatly on whether the Packers won or lost. I remember going downstairs to the basement of the (party) house, and finding Jerry Kramer (Green Bay Packers 1958-1968) sitting on a table with his broken ankle elevated. Jerry had broken the ankle on a kick-off, a few games earlier in the season. Jerry was like Paul Hornung in that, he was very talented and could play many different positions on the team. This would be one of many times I would run into him and… Jerry is a special person to me. I think we like each other because we have mutual interests, like hunting and fishing, and we have discussed how much we like certain parts of the some of same books… like Michener's, "**<u>Chesapeake</u>**," and the words of Rod McKuen's poetry. (Rod McKuen was a popular poet and songwriter in the 1960's and was an acquaintance of Jerry. McKuen is still around) Jerry gave little, pontificating lectures to me (he gives those frequently), about the fact that sooner or later, I needed to get <u>serious</u> about my life and go to college. I remember telling him in about 1963, I had <u>finally</u> decided to go to college at the University of Wisconsin-

Oshkosh. "Absolutely, NOT!" he said, discouraging me.
"Whyyyyy?" I whined, desiring his approval and listening to his
advice. "Because Oshkosh is <u>too</u> close to Green Bay, and for
you that means **too** close to **temptation**. You'll <u>never</u> make it,
if you go to Oshkosh!" He was right! As I said, when I lived in
Milwaukee I would party and end up driving to Green Bay late
at night. It was a 90-mile trip… and I would sober up, and then,
have to drive back in the morning. How much easier and more
tempting it would be, if I lived in Oshkosh… half the distance.

Two years later I decided to try college at the University of
Wisconsin-Stevens Point. In the early '60's I started college at
least six times, only to quit because of another party invitation
which I did not want to refuse. I thought Stevens Point would
be safer for me because it is about 50 miles further away from
Green Bay, than Oshkosh.

On Monday nights after 1965, **<u>nothing</u>** could stop me from
driving to Appleton to be at Fuzzy Thurston's **Left Guard,** bar
and restaurant, to party with my beloved, Green Bay Packers.
<u>NOTHING</u>! I remember being <u>extra</u> cautious because Highway

10, the road between Stevens Point and Appleton, was narrow, dark, and heavily populated with deer. I did <u>not</u> hit any, but on several occasions I certainly came close. I partied with the Packers every Monday night during football season from 1965 until 1968. We would gather, drink, and dance until closing, and we'd sing the song, "Once Upon a Time There Was a Tavern…. Those were the days, my friend, we thought they'd never end…. we'd sing and laugh forever and a day. We'd live the life we'd choose… we'd fight and <u>never lose</u>. Those were the days. Oh, **yes**, <u>those were the days</u>." Do you remember it? Then Fuzzy would sing, "He's Got the Whole World in His Hands." Fuzzy got throat cancer a few years later and had to have his larynx removed, and those of us who <u>love</u> him, probably miss his singing most of all! Once in awhile he still tries to belt one out, and to us, it is the ***sweetest*** music!

In those years at the end of the evening, if one was "lucky," one might get to go home with a "prince charming." Not exactly <u>HOME</u>, but you know <u>what</u> I mean. Remember the old saying, "You have to kiss a lot of toads before you find Prince Charming." Believe me! I did a lot of <u>kissing</u>! I think I was

127

placed into the category of "available single girl," but I suppose I could have been called a "groupie" or a "camp-follower" or, the more modern term, a "jersey-chaser," but I never felt like one. I always felt as though I belonged, probably because the fellows treated me kindly and with their own version of <u>respect</u>. Hard to imagine, RIGHT? But by the late 1960's I had been around for a long time, and I had so many good friends who were Packers players, few people considered me anything other than "one of the 'guys.'" Recently, Boyd Dowler mentioned how <u>special</u> those Glory Days had been, and reminded me that I had been <u>a part of it all</u>. I already knew I had been <u>a part of it all,</u> but it is nice to know he recognized it, too. After all, that is really what I always wanted to be... <u>a part of it</u>! The Packers of that era, to the present day, are like the brothers I never had! And some of them are still looking out for me... Ron Kramer, Dan Currie, Jerry Kramer, Boyd Dowler, Donny Anderson, Bob Long, Willie Wood, Fuzzy, and, *"yes, you guessed it"* ....even PAUL! Thanks, fellows!

Back to the Championship game-

We won! We beat the New York Giants by the unbelievable score of 37-0. It was a super, action-packed game for the Packers. The Giants did **not** have a good day! The Packers were ready… it was their turn and they knew it…so did the crowd and for that matter, so did the Giants! The cold air of Green Bay was charged with electricity you could actually feel! The game was particularly enjoyable for Coach Lombardi because his present team was whipping the tar out of his former team. Paul had recently been drafted into the Army, but, the military allowed him to come home to Green Bay from Kansas to play. Pvt. Paul Hornung was spectacular and his performance dominated the Giants. The Packers stole four passes from Y.A. Tittle, the Giant's quarterback, and made it all look so easy! People were already calling Green Bay, "TITTLETOWN," instead of Titletown, indicating that Y.A. Tittle was giving Green Bay the title. They were also chanting, "Sam Huff" (a New York Giant defensive lineman) "is on his duff!" The Giants were simply, out-classed. They had some early chances but blew all of them. I remember N.Y. Giant great, Kyle Rote, another one of my boyfriends, dropped a sure touchdown pass. (I gave up dating him because I felt that by dating a N.Y. Giant,

I was cheating on the Green Bay Packers, and I was. Right?)
The people in the stadium went crazy and they cheered and
hollered when a halfback for the Giants, missed an easy chance
to hit Kyle Rote in the end-zone. Starr threw touchdowns to
Ron Kramer and Boyd Dowler and then, Paul kicked a field
goal just before the half. In the second half, Ron Kramer (THE
TANK) (That's what they called him then) connected with a
pass from Starr, and then… Paul kicked two <u>more</u> field goals
and ended it. It was <u>over</u>, and for the first time in 17 years, <u>The
Green Bay Packers</u> were the <u>Champions of the World</u>. Hooray!

The crowd was uncontrollable… everyone was hugging…
and kissing… and hollering. They tore down the goalposts and
dragged them out of Lambeau Field. Somehow, they managed
to put them back up in downtown Green Bay near Main and
Adams Streets, and all the tavern doors were swung open.
People had to be crowded through the front door of the taverns
and then, had to leave by the back door. It was really <u>cold,</u> but
you would never know it from the way people were dressed, or
behaved. There was one bar next to the Northland Hotel which
was chucker-block-full of people. When Bill and I finally got

inside, Bart Starr was on stage, singing for the crowd. I think he may have been drinking a little champagne, but don't quote me. (Bart does not drink) Anyhow, he introduced his young back-up quarterback, John Roach, and it became obvious John had been drinking more than a <u>little</u> champagne. He slurred words to the crowd something like these: "Ladies and gentlemen! I made <u>five</u> <u>thousand</u> <u>dollars</u> today… and I <u>did</u> it… sitting on my **<u>ASS</u>**!" Of course, it was the truth. He had not left the bench because Bart Starr had controlled the field that day, and the crowd went <u>wild</u> with laughter and cheering.

After that, Bill and I made our way down to Speed's. I knew some of the Packers would end up there, and sure enough, there was Dapper Dan Currie. He immediately grabbed me, hugged me, and gave me a big, championship kiss. I hung on to Dan for the rest of the evening because I knew I would be safe with him and I might see Paul… Paul and Dan are good friends. Also, if I stuck with Dan I might get in on some private Packer-player parties, later that night. Bill stayed with us until 2:00 A.M. and none of the bars closed, I think by order of the Mayor and City Council, or perhaps, because none of the authorities had the heart to close them. They were probably celebrating the event themselves.

It is obvious the citizens of Green Bay love their Packers. One of the fun stories about how they take care of the players is told by Dave Robison (Green Bay Packers 1967-1972) during the ICE BOWL. When Dave got outside on that frigid Sunday morning to leave for Lambeau Field, his car would not start. (After all, it was 10 degrees below zero.) He had to hitch a ride to the stadium from a neighbor, but when the game was over and he came out, there was his car, all warmed up for him. Someone had taken the time to get it started and a couple of folks probably pitched in to get it to the stadium for Dave.

Bill asked me if I wanted to go home. Was he **crazy**? No way! Bill was tired and left, but he said I should call him at the house where we were staying… if I needed him. Good guy! Dan and I partied hardy, and at the end of the evening we went back to a motel (I think it was the Downtowner) where he was rooming with someone. "*Yes… you guessed it!*" He was rooming with Paul Hornung and someone else was staying with them also, but I never figured out who it was… they never returned to the room. The minute Dan got into the motel room, he fell asleep. Guess it had been a big day! Well, I should think so!

On the nightstand between the beds, I saw an opened letter addressed to Paul Hornung. (Paul, I must confess, temptation got the better of me and I read it.) ("*Read the letter…if you must, but hurry up about it*!") It was a love letter to Paul from the socialite in Milwaukee. Gee, was it ever juicy! I had my eyes opened to what girls would do to land Paul Hornung. She said she was **really** in <u>love</u> with him… Big deal! So was I, and I wanted to tell Paul that … I was the **really** <u>right</u> girl for him. Couldn't he see that? The big dumbie! I put the letter back where I found it, and not any too soon, because a few seconds later the door opened and in came Paul. He was very darling and very drunk. He immediately called me "Honey," which sounded to me like, "I love you truly." He grabbed my hand and said he had been looking for me all evening. Of course he had! Remember, we did not have cell phones to track each other down, so naturally I believed him. Who was I to doubt Paul

Hornung! I congratulated him on his great performance in the game. He was loving, and obviously, wanted to perform again. I remember saying something about… not knowing how to do the things he most likely wanted me to do. Remember, I had just read this juicy letter from his girlfriend, and I was again feeling insecure and inadequate. Well, Paul was unstoppable that day! He kissed me and told me I was just perfect the way I was. Of course! He said what I didn't know about sex, he would teach me. He said he would instruct me on how to make love to him, just the way he liked it. REALLY? WOW! I was hoping he meant he was going to show me right now … but after all it had been a long day. Anyhow, he did what boys do… and promptly fell asleep. To this day, I don't know what Paul wanted me to do and I will never know because Paul is happily married to a beautiful Italian girl… but I must admit that 40+ years later, I still wonder!

All of us woke up about the same time, and I will never forget the surprised expression on Dan Currie's face when he looked over and saw me in the other bed with Paul. I am sure he figured he missed something but wasn't sure what. Dan said he would see all of us later at church (yes, church), but right now, he had to go pick up a car which he had purchased for his younger brother, Michael. He was going to take it on the ferry from Manitowoc, WI to Ludington, MI that afternoon. Dan lived in Detroit.

It was New Year's morning! Happy New Year! Paul asked me where I had been staying for the weekend. I explained it all to him and with that, I called Bill and asked him to come and get me. I figured it was time to exit the scene before I became <u>excess</u> baggage and got in the way. It is **wise** to know **when** it is **time** to leave… and to **leave**. Bill picked me up and we went back to the house to get my belongings. It was a Holy Day so we went to the Catholic Church for Mass. The church was crowded and we had to stand up in the back, and it seemed as though everyone in Green Bay was in attendance… not only because of the Holy Day, but, everyone wanted to thank the Lord… for the Packer victory. Seriously! It was sheer coincidence, but standing in the back of the church, though I had left them at the motel only an hour before, were Dan Currie and Paul Hornung. We grinned when we saw each other, and Paul edged closer and nudged me. I think Ron Kramer was there, too! A few moments later a cloud of fatigue came over me and I felt sick. Staying up all night, drinking, and the excitement of it all had finally hit me. I backed up and leaned against the Confessional. I was startled by a <u>low</u> groan coming from inside the confessional box…. it sounded as though someone was dying in there. I pulled open the curtain and there sat the ubiquitous, Wild Bill Quinlan… and he looked awful. "Oh, my God, Bill!" I exclaimed. He grinned and said, "HI YA, SNAPPA!"

When Mass ended we bid our farewells and departed for our respective homes. It was a new year… **we** were the Champions of the whole world, and our hearts were filled with the excitement and anticipation of the football season to come.

This photo always made me smile when I needed to. I usually had it posted on my door so I could see it before I left to go somewhere I did not want to go...like...to work. (L. to R.) Dan Currie, Paul Hornung, Bart Starr, and Ron Kramer. (Credit: Milwaukee Sentinel)

Sandy Sullivan

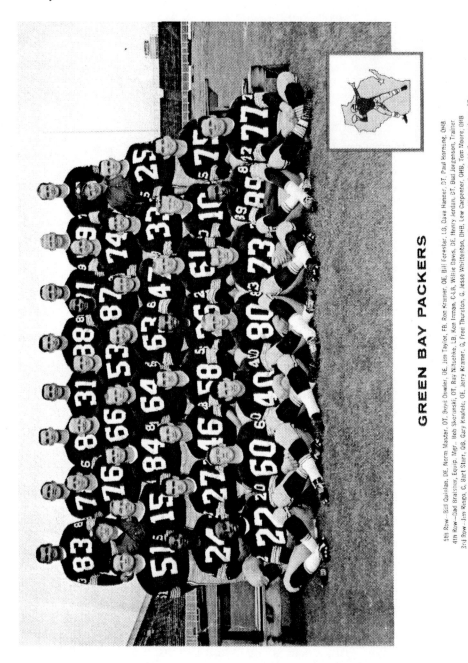

1962 Team Photo by Laughhead Photographers, Dallas, Texas
(copyright-1962)

138

1962 GREEN BAY PACKERS

Photo by Laughead Photographers, Dallas, Texas (copyright 1962) from the personal collection of Dan Currie with permission. The initials DC are imprinted by the photographer on the back of the photo. This picture was taken seconds after the official team photo above. Incidentally, Paul Hornung wants credit for this photo because he says it is he who got the team to horse around for the photographer. Thanks, Paul!

WILD BILL

The Green Bay Packers have had many characters play for them, and one who stands out in my mind is Bill Quinlan (Green Bay Packers 1959-1962). The following headline appeared in a local newspaper when Bill was returning to play in the Canadian Football League: "FATHERS, LOCK UP YOUR DAUGHTERS, WILD BILL RETURNS." No headline could better forewarn and explain the ebullient presence of Wild Bill.

Bill Quinlan is a graduate of Michigan State University. He played football there shortly before Dan Currie. In fact, Bill and Dan look somewhat alike. Both have black hair, are about 6'3" tall, and weigh about 240 lbs. The main difference in appearance is that Bill has a larger head than Dan. In pro-ball, Bill played defensive end and Dan played defensive linebacker. Danny is Irish and Polish, and Bill Quinlan is Irish and German. Anyone who knows about the ethnic mixture of Irish and German knows how volatile it can sometimes become. On occasion, the good folks of Green Bay mistook Dan Currie for Bill Quinlan, and Dan would get blamed for Bill's shenanigans. Bill is from Lawrence, <u>MASSACHUSETTS</u> and speaks with a very pronounced New England <u>Yankee</u> twang. His favorite expression when greeting a female was to refer to her as "SNAPPA." He had a crude habit of greeting women by saying, "Howaya, howaya, howaya! How's your (w)hole… (*gasp!*)… (pause)… FAMILY." (*Oh, my Lord!*)

To understand what I mean when I say Bill Quinlan's a <u>character</u> let me begin by telling a story about Bill and the tavern he owned. Lawrence, MA is a blue-collar town where Bill ran a profitable neighborhood pub near the factories. His accountant met with him one day and told him there was a problem. It appeared someone was siphoning money out of Bill's business. Sometimes the deficit was as much as $500 per day. "How do ya' think I can catch the rotten bastard?" asked Bill. "Well, if I were <u>you</u>," replied the accountant. "I would get a private detective to watch <u>everything</u> that goes on and see who is stealing from you." Bill Quinlan was upset about the theft and upon the suggestion of his accountant, he hired a private eye… and, for $1000 per month, the private-eye watched everything that went on in Bill's bar. When the month was up he reported his findings to Bill and the accountant. "The man responsible for the theft has dark hair… he has a very large head, weighs about 250 pounds, and is about six feet three inches tall and… he answers to the name of **<u>Bill</u>**." Bill would apparently get drunk, and later, have no recollection he was stealing his own money. It cost him $1000 to find out he was the thief, stealing from himself.

Bill Quinlan, like many good Irishmen, likes his whiskey. He drank a lot and in the early 60's, Vince Lombardi became concerned with Bill's drinking <u>problem</u>. Let me add here… Lombardi saw it as a "problem" …Bill did not! Cautiously, Lombardi approached Bill and said, "Bill, you have to slow down. You are going to have to change your lifestyle." Bill asked whose lifestyle he should follow. "How about mine, Bill?" replied Lombardi. Bill did what Lombardi asked. He stopped drinking his usual amount of whiskey and within a week, had lost 10 lbs and became ill. So ill in fact, he was ordered to bed, with the possibility of being hospitalized. Lombardi sent a physician to examine him, and the physician said the <u>sudden</u> abstinence had been a shock to Bill's body. Finally, Lombardi himself went to visit. Bill ranted and raved, "You see, Coach! You asked me to change my lifestyle to your lifestyle, and it damned near killed me." To which Lombardi replied, "I can see that, Bill, and I promise, I will <u>never</u> ask you to change your lifestyle again." Bill resumed his former habits, and within a week was well enough to play football.

One time after a game in the County Stadium-Milwaukee, I met Bill and his friend partying in a nightclub called the Holiday House, in Milwaukee's downtown area. Hornung was there at the piano bar singing "Just a Gigolo, Everywhere I go." The ladies were making passes at him, but, he asked me to have breakfast with him after the bar closed. It was Sunday night and the players did not have to return to practice in Green Bay until

Tuesday morning.

I have heard that Monday is <u>not</u> the day <u>off</u> for the <u>present</u> Packer team, but in **my** day… the "**day to play**" was Monday. I ended up planning my modeling schedule, and later on, my college classes, so I would be free to party with my beloved Packers on Mondays.

A lot of the players were at the Holiday House and we partied until the nightclub closed, and then, a bunch of us went to have breakfast together at an all-night restaurant. By 6:00 A.M. the teammates were deciding where they would spend their day off. Paul decided he would go with some players; Jesse Whittenton and others, to play golf at Lawsonia Country Club in Green Lake. He asked Bill when he was planning to return to Green Bay, and Bill said he was leaving in a little while. Paul asked me if I wanted to ride up to Green Bay with Bill and his friend, and meet <u>him</u> later that evening. Of course, I said, "YES!"

With no sleep we left for Green Bay after Bill's friend

checked out of the Astor Hotel. We had the friend's car and she was driving. Bill bought a couple of six-packs for the trip. The friend's name was Mary and I think Mary was happy to have me ride along, because Bill was wild! He wanted to stop at every bar between Milwaukee and Green Bay. By late afternoon, I could tell Mary was anxious to get home and she inevitably, started to speed. A Wisconsin Highway Patrolman pulled us over near the Little Chute Exit on Highway 41. Bill, vehemently, announced he would handle the situation, and we were ordered to stay in the car and keep our mouths shut. He jumped out of the car and proceeded to tell the patrolman his name, saying he was a member of the World Champion Green Bay Packers. Then he said in his Yankee twang, "So, Officer, because you are a member of the Highway Patrol of the great State of Wisconsin, I am going to give you free tickets to next Sunday's game in Green Bay." "Well, thank you, Bill," said the cop. "I appreciate your gesture…. and…. because I am a member of the Highway Patrol of the great State of Wisconsin, here is Mary's **free** ticket." Bill solemnly returned to the car. When the door closed, you should have heard him yell. "That no-good, rotten, SON of a Bitch! To think I gave that S.O.B. my free tickets to next Sunday's game. The dirty rotten #&*@##@, S. O. B.!!!!!!" It was quiet in the car for the rest of the way. I met up with Paul later that evening, and on Tuesday morning, I took a Greyhound bus back to Milwaukee.

One time I left my car in the Northland Hotel parking lot, and my friends and I were given a ride over to Speed's. As the evening grew late, I decided it was time for me to get my car and pick up my friends. Not visualizing the ramifications, I asked Bill if he would kindly give me a <u>lift</u> to my car. "OF COURSE, I WILL, SNAPPA." With that, he picked me up, threw me over his right shoulder, and carried me for five blocks. I was scared to death he would drop me or maybe drag me into the bushes. I didn't know what to expect... he was unpredictable... what could one expect from a man who had purchased a real live pony, and had led it into the Maternity Ward to give to his newborn son? So, I did not make any waves, and he engaged me in a normal conversation during the journey, and I conversed with him calmly as if we were walking side-by-side. But we were not side-by-side, and all the while we were talking during this journey, I was staring into the back, right-hand, wallet-pocket of his trousers; big butt and all. When we arrived at my car he nonchalantly turned me upright, standing me on my feet, and straightening my dress for me. With relief I said, "Oh, thank you, Bill!" "YOU'RE WELCOME, SNAPPA!" and off he went, and I never saw him again! However, that does not mean he disappeared. To the contrary! Bill Quinlan is <u>larger</u> than life… how could anyone like Bill become lost, disappear, or be forgotten? Bill was traded from the Green Bay Packers to the Philadelphia Eagles in 1963, and then to the Detroit Lions in 1964. He ended his pro-football career in 1965, playing for the Washington Redskins.

When I think of Bill I am immediately reminded of his very-heavy Yankee accent. Words of the English Language which you and I say and hear with standard English-American pronunciation, simply do <u>not</u> come out of Bill Quinlan the same way. For example, when we say, "…we were "partying," meaning to go out and have fun at a gathering and so forth… Bill would say the same words, and they would come out sounding like "…we were **<u>pottying</u>.**" Go ahead now… say it out loud so you get my drift. That's right. You've got it!

Pottying! "Pottying" means <u>partying</u> to you and me and to most other Americans… and believe me, Bill loved to **"<u>potty</u>"**.

At the time, the owner of the Washington Redskins was Edward Bennett Williams, a prominent D.C. attorney, who had taken pride in using his fortune and prestige to assemble the finest football team money could buy. Williams' strategy was to acquire pro-football players and coaches who had personally experienced championships. For personnel he wanted only those who knew what it felt like to win, and those who knew how to get there. Isn't that what all owners want, if they can get it? But it takes more than just the winning <u>experience</u> to win ball games, as Williams found out. His team was losing and he wanted to know <u>why</u>. Williams gathered his coaching staff and players, asking them if they were aware of the effort and finances he had rendered in an attempt to produce a <u>winning</u> Redskins team. Everyone nodded with understanding, as if they had a clue. Then he desperately put forth a profound question… Could any one of them, considering their combined years of experience, come up with a <u>reason</u> **<u>why</u>** they were <u>not</u> winning? Anyone? Williams looked around the room at blank faces. Then with no particular preference in mind, he picked Bill Quinlan and said, "How about <u>you</u>, Billy? Can **you** think of a <u>reason</u>… **why** we're **not** winning?"

Always the "showman," and deeply honored that Williams had singled him out, Bill stood up, threw back his mighty shoulders, raised his noble chin, stepped to the front of the room, and addressed the men. "Mr. Edward Bennett Williams, visionary and benefactor of the Washington Redskins… … esteemed head coach… honored coaching staff… my fellow teammates. Gentlemen! (LOUDLY) **It is my humble opinion that the reason we are not <u>winning</u> is because there is not <u>enough</u> "<u>POTTYING</u>" going on!** The room went wild! Edward Bennett Williams laughed and said, "Bill, you may be <u>right</u>! Everyone get out of here and go "potty" for a few days." They did! And sure enough, the next Sunday, the Redskins won. What a genius!

There is a good lesson to be learned here… if you're not winning, perhaps, you are working <u>too</u> hard, and need to do a little partying. You know what they say …all work and no play …makes Jack a dull boy! (Of course, they also say…all work and no play, makes JACK!) Regardless, Bill Quinlan is definitely not a <u>dull</u> boy, so I am <u>sure</u>, wherever he is… he is still "pottying." God love him!

<u>Update!</u>

"Of all the gin joints in the world you had to walk into mine…" said Humphrey Bogart meeting Ingrid Bergman in "<u>Casablanca</u>." Well… there are now 72,000+ seats in Lambeau field, and I went to the dedication of the new stadium in September 2003. Of all the seats I could have gotten in the entire stadium, I walked in and sat down right next to Bill Quinlan. I had not seen him in over 40 years, and I was thunderstruck! He looks terrific! I told him about the story I was writing about Wild Bill. He blushed and told me he had not had a drink in over 20 years. He said that <u>Wild Bill</u> no longer exists, and we must call him "<u>Sweet William</u>" now. Okay, Bill, you've got it! "<u>Sweet William</u>" it is! …"Here's looking at <u>you</u>, kid!"

CHAMPIONSHIP GAME – NUMBER 2

The 1962 Championship game was played in New York City. The Packers played the Giants again, for the second year in a row… and this time the Packers won, 16-7. I watched the game on television, but of course I wanted to be there… I had never been to New York City.

I was tickled when my linebacker friend, Dan Currie, intercepted a pass and headed for the Packer end zone. I screamed, "Go, Danny, go!" Dan said he watched the ball, deflected by Nitschke, go so high into the air he had time to say three Our Fathers and three Hail Marys before it came down. He was praying he would catch it! Then he wanted to hand it to Willie Wood, who he knew could run it back for the touchdown.

However, Willie ran by Dan like a shot from a cannon, and so, Dan had to run with the ball. But, the long run was not to be! (Incidentally, Ray Nitschke won the MVP award and Paul Hornung was also a hero that day. Paul was given many awards and trophies in those days. I once heard someone gave him a mink-lined, jock strap embroidered, "To Paul Hornung of the Green Bay Peckers." I am not sure if this is true, but I think it is.) (*Don't quote me.*)

Unfortunately for Dan, he hit a patch of ice and his feet went out from under him. The game was being played in Yankee Stadium and the baselines, on the still-existing baseball diamond, were slick with ice. Everything in New York was frozen that day. Even the film in the NFL Films, Inc. cameras was freezing and breaking. Dan tells, that while running down the sidelines past the Packer bench, he could hear Fuzzy Thurston hollering at him. "Go, Danny! Go, Danny! GO!" Then, Dan's feet flew out from under him and he could hear Fuzzy yelling, "No, Danny, No! You dumb Son of a Bitch." Fuzzy had gone from cheering him to cursing him in less than 10 seconds.

A couple of years ago I was at Fuzzy's establishment, on Mason Street in Green Bay, visiting with some of my dear, Packer friends. They were in town doing a promotion for the Lombardi Legend's Charity Group. Fuzzy, Ron Kramer, Boyd Dowler, and I were in the front room of the bar with Fuzzy's grandson, Joey, watching the film of this 1962 Championship game. We were having a great time mimicking Chris Schinkle, the sport commentator, who was vehemently describing a run Ron Kramer was making. He said, "**<u>Rugged Ron sheds Giants like ducks shed water</u>**!" (*Try saying that fast… I dare you!*) At the end of the film, Fuzzy was standing like a gladiator on the field in front of the passageway to the locker rooms, talking with a referee who was holding a football. Finally, the referee handed the football to Fuzzy. Fuzzy had made a case to the referee that the game ball should belong to him. Leave it to Fuzzy! His <u>love</u> for the game and the effort it had taken to win the championship should be commemorated with a memento. Right? This is a great example of what Fuzzy is all about, and what things like <u>this</u> mean to him. It's all about <u>love</u>! Ron asked Fuzzy what happened to the football, and Fuzzy said he still has it.

After a lot of begging, Boyd Dowler once gave me an autographed football of Super Bowl I. It was left in the original cardboard box in which it had come. I wanted to save it to give to **my** grandchildren. When I moved to Connecticut in 1987, one of the movers stole it. (*Are you reading this now, you thief? If so, shame on you! I hope this book costs you $1000. My football must be worth that by now. If anyone in Connecticut has seen this football… you know where it came from and who it belongs to. I am offering a reward for stealing it back! Get out of this man's house immediately, and check your pockets before you leave!*)

Dan Currie intercepts a ball deflected by Ray Nitschke during the 1962 Championship Game on December 30th in Yankee Stadium, New York. Baselines of the Yankee Baseball diamond are iced over. Dan wanted to give the ball to Willie Wood, but Willie went by him like a shot from a cannon. Jesse Whittenton #47 looks on and I think NY Giants # 85, is Del Shofner. From the collection of Dan Currie with permission.

This is a photo of the same play, taken from the sidelines.
Championship Game #2, 12/30/62, New York: Yankee Stadium
Photo from the collection of Vernon Biever (copyright)

Dan Currie runs toward the Green Bay end zone. Note: Jesse
Whittenton #47 follows, while Willie Wood #24 looks to clear a
path. Herb Adderley #26 throws a block on NY Giant #62. New York
Giant #55 is Ray Wietecha, and #79 is Roosevelt Brown. From the
collection of Dan Currie with permission.

CREATE YOUR OWN DESTINY

Write a letter…and as a <u>direct</u> result….be inducted into the Professional Football **Hall of Fame**! Is it possible? "No!" Well, I <u>know</u> it's possible because my friend, Willie Wood, did it. (Green Bay Packers 1960-1971) His… is one of the greatest success stories I have ever heard, and from it I learned that creativity enables us to enter and re-enter life.

Many people do not know Willie Wood was the first <u>black</u> quarterback in U.S. College Football history. Not only was he the quarterback, playing on offense, but he had the ability to switch and play the position of defensive back. When he completed his college football career at the University of Southern California - Los Angeles (USC), he was looking

161

forward to playing in the NFL. But guess what? Nobody wanted a running, black quarterback. At the time black quarterbacks were not (for want of a better word) *"welcome"* in the NFL. But Willie Wood was <u>not</u> to be denied his destiny! He studied all the NFL teams, looking for weaknesses in personnel where his talent could be utilized and provide strength. He wrote <u>only</u> three letters asking for a chance to try out, addressing them to the <u>General Manager</u> of the San Francisco 49er's, the N.Y. Giants, and the Green Bay Packers. He received <u>only</u> ***one*** reply…and, it was from Vince Lombardi. Lombardi invited Willie Wood to Green Bay for a try-out with the Packers. Willie was asked to jump and touch the cross-bar on the goal post. He is 5' 10" tall, but he did this with ease and grace, and Lombardi immediately recognized Willie's athletic ability. It did not take long before for he put Willie on defense, where he was <u>soon</u> recognized as an excellent free safety. In his second year with Green Bay he became a starter (1961), and he did not leave this position until he retired eleven years later. In the course of eight years, beginning in 1964 until he retired, he received all-pro honors <u>every</u> year. In other words, he participated in the Pro-Bowl eight times and played in six NFL championship games. "In Super Bowl I and II he was the starting <u>free safety</u>. One of his greatest achievements came in Super Bowl I, when the Packers were playing the Kansas City Chiefs, and the score was close in the third quarter. Willie intercepted a pass thrown by Len Dawson and… went 50 yards… The spectacular play (relieved Lombardi's stress level) and started a rally which steamrolled the Packers to a 35-10 victory." (Carroll - 1998) Most people think that Willie Wood went all the way for the touchdown, but it was Elijah Pitts who took the ball into the end zone from the 6 yard line.

I have spoken with some of the other Packer players about Willie's ability. Boyd Dowler says that Willie plays football with "street smarts." "He surveys the entire set-up and always anticipates every player's next move. It's like he has a sixth sense and anticipates exactly, what the other fellow is going to do before he does it." Perhaps this skill and ability comes from growing up in urban Washington, D.C. where one, at a very young age, develops a heightened observance of physical surroundings. To this day he will not sit with his back to the door.

Many people (men in particular*)* assume football players, or for that matter all athletes, get their athletic <u>ability</u> from their <u>fathers</u>, but Willie Wood readily says he got his… from his <u>mother</u>. Both he and his mother went to Washington, D.C. Armstrong High School, where his mother was an <u>outstanding</u> basketball player. In later years his elderly, athletic mother was active with the D.C. Recreation Centers and participated in many track and marathon events. The same is true of Boyd Dowler's <u>mother</u> who was a basketball and track star at the University of Wyoming. Boyd says his father probably took one look at his mother and said, "WOW, I'm gonna' have me some <u>sons</u>!" …and he did!

There is a fun and interesting story about Boyd Dowler, who grew up in Cheyenne, WY and where his buddies set up a race between a quarter horse and him... Boyd beat the horse. That's where my money would have been... on Boyd! He was creating his own destiny, just like Willie.

So go ahead… I dare you! Create your own destiny! Willie

did! …and in the summer of 1989, William Vernell (Willie) Wood, happily journeyed to Canton, OH to be inducted into the Professional Football **Hall of Fame…** all because he believed in himself, and had taken the time to write a few letters.

The wonderful face of Pro-Football Hall of Fame member, Willie Wood. Taken by the author in Northern Wisconsin, December, 1998.

OUT OF THE

STARTING LINE-UP

One day, while <u>still</u> working at the modeling agency in Milwaukee, I received a phone call. The fellow calling said his name was Lee Walls. He also said he played for the Los Angeles Dodgers, and had gotten my number from Paul Hornung. OUCH! That hurt! I was devastated, but I should have expected it. I had been dropped from Paul Hornung's starting line-up... I was no longer on his A-list. Perhaps I had never been on it! I imagined all sorts of scenarios, like Paul handing this fellow a match-book cover which read:

"For a good time - CALL SANDY!"

As it turned out, that is **not exactly** what Paul did.
Apparently the two had met in a Chicago night club, and Walls
said he was going to Milwaukee to play baseball, and asked
Paul to suggest a young lady with whom he might get a date.
BINGO! Lucky me! My name was drawn from a <u>full</u> pot!
Paul's little black book was thicker than "War and Peace." Paul
suggested <u>me</u>, and now you're probably thinking this is just as
terrible as handing over a match-book cover. Thinking about it
now, I have to agree. But when you're 19 years old… don't give
a darn…and are pretty naive… you think this means you're
"<u>popular</u>." Besides, Paul probably thought he was doing all of
us a favor by introducing us. It was high time I learned how to
play in this fast-paced ballgame. Right? Only Paul Hornung can
tell us what he actually told Lee Walls about me, and I doubt
if he remembers. But my guess is that Paul opened his "black
book" to the final page, and since my last name was "Young" at
the time, I was on the last page in the "X-Y-Z" section. Could

be! This is pure speculation, and besides, it doesn't matter to me now, as much as it once did.

Lee Walls turned out to be a fine fellow! I liked him… even if he was a <u>baseball</u> player. He was knowledgeable and I learned from him. I remember he used big words like "contiguous," and I liked the word and took it for my own vocabulary. Every time I have used the word since, I am reminded of Lee Walls. I have a good memory and I remember little things like… words… and sayings! Some fellows most likely think I remember them for their physical prowess, like guys remember women, but I don't. (To explain what I mean about guys remembering women… there is a famous hockey player who was asked for the most vivid and exciting <u>memory</u> of his long and illustrious sports career, and after a moment's pause he said, "It would have to be that <u>redhead</u> in Cleveland.") As for me, I remember particular incidences and special things which were said and done. For example, Paul once told me it was a good idea to leave my window open at night when I went to bed. He said the fresh air was good for me. Of course I did as he suggested, but I questioned this because at the time, my bedroom window faced the Milwaukee Industrial Valley, and every morning I had an inch of soot on my window sill. Paul didn't know about pollution in 1961. About a month later, a woman who lived a few blocks from me, was beaten and raped. The intruder had come through her <u>open</u> bedroom window. I stopped listening to Paul ... he could have gotten me killed! ... And, this is for the lady readers. Here's something which is very important if you are planning to run around with a professional athlete. Learn to have your hair and make-up <u>perfect</u>, be dressed, and ready to go when the fellow is ready to leave. If you take <u>too</u> long he will leave without you. Also, look your ***best***, otherwise, some little <u>dolly</u> will out-woman you, and it will be all <u>your</u> fault. Be prepared and look great! Oh, and ...also... don't <u>forget</u> anything. You are <u>not</u> going to have an opportunity to <u>go back</u> and get it. I credit Dan Currie for teaching me this. I used to take forever to get ready or leave something behind. Finally Dan said, if I wanted to go with him, I had better learn to remember things and hustle, or be left. He asked me how it would look if an athlete left something behind, or missed the kick-off. Gee Whiz! He made perfect sense. He was right. I never wanted to miss out on anything, so,

I practiced and I learned to spring into action on a moment's notice. This valuable information probably saved my marriage a few times. My husband loved to go to the race track, and, if you have a horse going off in the first race, you had better be there <u>in</u> <u>time</u> to get your bet in. Now, here's more important poop! And this is <u>dangerous</u>…so listen up! If you <u>really</u> <u>want</u> to irritate your husband or boyfriend, giving him grounds for divorce … try dill-dallying around, making him really late for the <u>First Race</u>. Even worse… because of <u>you</u>… he <u>misses</u> the first race <u>completely</u>, and his horse **<u>wins</u>**. (*OH, my Lord! This happened to me and I'm lucky to be alive to tell you of my tale. Come to think of it, if the horse <u>lost</u>, it would be <u>my</u> fault, too. Why is everything <u>my</u> fault?*) But, you know what? The men are absolutely RIGHT! There is **<u>no</u>** excuse for being late! So get with the program, Dover, and "move your bloomin' arse!"

Another incident I remember was the time in '63, when I was making love with a World Champion St. Louis Cardinal (The Cardinals had just won the World Series). This particular <u>champion</u> was a gum-chewer and, while making love, he got his gum stuck in my hair. His eyes got very dark and round and he said, "*OH! OH!*" He didn't know how to tell me and we laughed until we cried, and then we realized, there was no way to un-stick the gum and get it out, and I would have to cut my hair or shave my head. We went downstairs to a beauty salon on Rush Street (Chicago) and they shaved the hair off the left side of my head. Fun! *Oh, sure! For you, maybe! Not for me!* We had a ball trying to explain to the beautician just how the gum had ended up in my hair. Of course, it was pretty obvious how it happened!

This fellow was a real "HONEY" and he used the word "Bonita" for everything. Bonita means "beautiful" in Spanish, and, I suppose everything **is** "Bonita" when you have just won the World Series of Baseball. Another word he liked to use was "copasetic." This was a popular word in the early 60's, and it means everything is OKAY. Well, at Easter I made hard-boiled eggs, and I gave this funny, gum-chewing athlete, a hard-boiled egg, which I hand-painted with gold-metallic paint and then, inscribed it with the words…

"FOR LOTS OF COPASETIC BONITA LUCK"

It was a lucky charm and this sweetheart carried the egg in his duffle bag for most of the baseball season, <u>believing</u> it brought him good luck. At last, the egg accidentally fell on the floor in the St. Louis locker room and broke. The stench cleared the team from the facility, as each team member blamed another for the smell, accusing him of eating rotten eggs. I was told there was a good deal of cursing which accompanied the mass exodus. So much for my bright ideas and good luck charms.

Oh, yes! Lee Walls! (*Sorry! How quickly I forget!*)

He was an excellent conversationalist! At one time, he had worked at the ticket windows at Santa Anita Race Track, and had a bunch of stories he told me about the colorful characters at the track, and witnessing some really thrilling horse races. He was extremely interested in real estate, and as I recall, he was dabbling in California real estate investments. I have often wondered what happened to him, especially after he ended his baseball career. He always wanted the parcels of real estate to be **"<u>contiguous</u>,"** and I <u>hope</u> he lucked out!

Well, as you know, one thing leads to another! And, in the case of Lee Walls it led to something really <u>good</u>! His roommate! A very special person named Don Drysdale. In 1962, Don won the Cy Young Award and you probably already know that he is <u>now</u> a <u>legend</u> of baseball. I am proud to say he was my friend! In the summer of 1961, the Dodgers were playing the Milwaukee Braves at County Stadium. The Dodgers were staying at the Schroeder Hotel and Lee asked me to call him there. When I called his room, the gentleman who answered said Lee had been called back to California on an emergency, but Lee had asked him to meet me across the street at Fazio's and buy me a drink. Oh, goody!

What a treat! I walked in and met this great, big, beautiful, tan, giant of a man, with the softness of a stuffed toy bear. For some reason we clicked, and instantly became friends. Before I tell this story, I want to make something clear… Don Drysdale was a friend, never a lover… and I liked that arrangement just fine. He never got fresh and was always a perfect gentleman. When I agreed to meet him, I didn't know he was married and, while we sat at the bar I admired a beautiful, gold St.

Christopher medal he was wearing around his neck which was inscribed, "From G and K." I inquired who G and K were and he told me it stood for Ginger and Kelly, his wife and daughter. Gee! I was stunned! …and I didn't know what to say. He just grinned and said it was <u>okay</u>… he said he wasn't going to ask me to <u>marry</u> him. And…it **was** okay… because I was interested in marrying a football player, **not** a baseball player. (*Although, this guy would have been big enough to get me over the threshold.*)

Don Drysdale used to call me from various places when he was on the road, pitching. He was interested in how I was doing, and I knew he cared about what happened to me. I saw a lot more of him after I moved to Chicago. I don't know why exactly, but the Los Angeles Dodgers must have had more games in Chicago in the 1963 season. One of the things Don loved were the jokes I had learned while working in Chicago at the Domino Lounge. I had a wonderful repertoire of funny stories and had a great time telling them, and I enjoyed making the fellows laugh. Don would invite his teammates to Trader Vic's, downstairs in the Sheraton Hotel, where they were staying, and would ask me to come and entertain on afternoons when the game was rained out in Wrigley Field. I remember the Dodgers had a very successful year and I was always in awe of some of the famous players that Don would introduce to me. You'll likely call me a "name-dropper" but honestly, I really met all of these people through Don. There was handsome Sandy Koufax, and the Year's Most Valuable Player, Maury Wills. I remember meeting Johnny Podres, Ron Perranoski, and a huge fellow named Frank Howard.

One afternoon, Sandy Koufax, Johnny Podres, Frank Howard and some others showed up, and believe it or not, so did a curious Walter Alston, the manager. We all sat around and had a few laughs as I entertained them with my funny stories. But, this is the <u>best</u> part of all! Can you possibly guess <u>which</u> stories the Los Angeles Dodgers <u>really</u> wanted me to tell them? Can you guess? NO? Well… the stories the Los Angeles Dodgers really wanted to hear… were my stories about…

The Green Bay Packers.

Footnote: Don Drysdale was inducted into the Baseball Hall of Fame in 1984. He died of a massive coronary on July 3, 1993 in Montreal, Quebec, Canada. He was 57 years old. (*So long, old friend*!)

LOST WITH MCGEE

Several of the Green Bay Packers knew I worked at the Domino Lounge in Chicago. When they came to town to play the Bears, they stayed at the Drake Hotel, just down the street from the lounge. One night before a game some of the coaches stopped in, and Tom Fears, the coach for the ends and wide receivers was one of them.

The next summer in late August, I got a call at the lounge from Fears, asking if I had seen Max McGee. I was surprised and a little dumbfounded, and said, "No, I have not! Why?" ...I wondered **why** he was asking **me.** "Well, McGee hasn't shown up for training camp, and I thought perhaps you may have run into him in Chicago." Trying to be helpful, I asked if he had thought of calling Max's family in Texas, and Fears said he had already done that. "What did they say?" I inquired. "I got hold of Max's brother," said Fears, "and he said he had no idea where Max was. The brother said, 'Last I heard, Max was playing for some <u>football</u> team up in Wisconsin.'" I guess Texans just don't understand what we have going up here! I told Fears I would keep an eye-open for Max; and if I saw him, I would tell him to call Green Bay. (*HAH*! *There was a fat chance of **that** happening*!!!) Fears yelled, "If you see him…**tell him to get his <u>ASS</u> up here…! Lombardi is really <u>steamed</u>!**"

A couple of nights later, I was having dinner at a restaurant on Rush Street. It was owned by a great friend of mine by the name of Tommy Downs. Tommy was one of the most respected restaurateurs in Chicago. He always seated me in the front window so I could look up and down Rush Street while I dined. I watched a couple approaching me… and …I couldn't believe my eyes. Along strolled Max McGee with a really, tall doll on his arm… a "break-your-neck looker." People on the street were turning to look at her as they passed. She was <u>so blonde</u> and <u>so beautiful</u> she took <u>my</u> breath away, too! I went out and said,

"Max, it's <u>ME</u>... <u>Sandy</u>. I got a call from Green Bay and they're <u>looking</u> for <u>you</u>." "That could very well be," Max said casually, "but... my fiancée and I have been doing a little traveling... and playing a little tennis." (*She was <u>not</u> his fiancée! Come on!*) As it turned out, the girl was a semi-pro tennis player who Max had met in Miami. Max drawled, "The old man (Lombardi) knows I'll show up ... <u>eventually</u>!"

I figured if Max wasn't worried, why should I be worried? Besides, I didn't want him to leave, not just yet... they wanted to party and so did I. So the three of us hung out for a day or so, and we hit all the saloons and nightclubs on Rush Street and around the Chicago Gold Coast. Max never seemed to mind if I came along... he was always <u>great</u> about that. I wish I could remember the girl's name ... I think it was Frankie or Teddy. She was a "real honey" and I picked her brain; asking for beauty tips and other important information a girl <u>needs</u> to know if they are going to catch a football star.

I never heard about this chance encounter again. I <u>know</u> the girl went back to Florida... I <u>know</u> I went back to work... and, I

<u>know</u> Max McGee went back to Green Bay because … well …
<u>I just know</u>.

THE SUCCESS OF WILLIE DAVIS

While living in Chicago I worked at the Domino Lounge which was a wonderful, little, upstairs lounge with great entertainment. I checked the coats in the winter months, and it was my job all of the time, to greet and seat the customers. Occasionally I sang songs and told jokes, and I committed to memory, most of the jokes the entertainers told. In the year or so that I worked there many famous entertainers stopped in and visited; Jonathon Winters, the comedian; Eddie Arnold, the late-great country western singer; and the late-great movie star, Caesar Romero, among others. Most likely, these are persons many of you are not familiar with. You are just, too darn young! For a while, one weekly-visitor was a Green Bay Packer by the name of Willie Davis (Green Bay Packers 1960-1969).

Willie was getting his MBA from the University of Chicago. He lived in Milwaukee but before driving home, he would stop and say <u>hello</u> to me at the lounge. Willie was working for the Schlitz Brewery in Milwaukee during the football off-season, and Schlitz was sponsoring him in his graduate program. After he got his degree, they made him a member of their Board of Directors and later, gave him the beer distributorship for the Los Angeles section of Watts.

Willie's teammate, Jerry Kramer (Green Bay Packers 1958-1968), made a film in the 1970's called "The Habit of Winning" which lauded his teammates for their successes on and off the football field. I remember one scene in which Jerry had Willie standing in front of a row of beer trucks which went on as far as the eye could see, and they all belonged to Willie. Jerry asked Willie if, when he was younger, he ever thought he would own all of these trucks, and Willie replied, "No, I thought I would be driving one."

Today, Willie Davis is a successful businessman and sits on the Board of Directors of many companies, and owns several radio stations. He was inducted into the Professional Football

Hall of Fame in 1981. A few months ago I received a phone call

from Spike Lee Studios in L.A. They were wondering if I knew

where to reach Willie Davis. Yes, I had that information! Lee

was doing a documentary on Jim Brown, the great full-back

of the Cleveland Browns, and wanted Willie Davis to be in it.

I was honored to be asked to locate Willie for the film. I saw

the documentary on HBO… it told of Jim Brown's struggles

and triumphs, and I knew that Willie Davis could write his own

book, and do a documentary about his <u>struggles</u> and fantastic

<u>triumph</u>s. Either one would be big hit!

Willie Davis signs a cap for a fan as Jerry Kramer looks on. Green
Bay, October 4,1998. Photo by Nick Martone, Las Vegas, NV

(From left to right) Jerry Kramer, Fuzzy Thurston #63 and Gale Gillingham #68, during Super Bowl II. Fuzzy did not play football until his junior year of college. For ten years he played left guard for Green Bay and helped them to five championship seasons. From the Collection of Vernon Biever (copyright)

(From left to right) Fuzzy Thurston, the author, and the late Tom Wiesner, University of Wisconsin Football great and NFL Alumni. Golf Tournament, July-1999, Spring Green, WI, NFL Alumni-Madison Chapter. The temperature was 105 degrees.

Fuzzy Thurston lends Jake Skall, Appleton, WI restaurateur and friend, his Super Bowl I ring to wear until his death, at Jake's 70th Birthday party. Jake signed everything with "Yours truly" because Jack Dempsey did.

THE GREAT FUZZEROO

<u>The following is Fuzzy Thurston's NFL History, in his own words:</u>

"Fuzzy Wuzzy was a <u>BEAR</u>, a grizzly bear.

Then Fuzzy Wuzzy became an <u>EAGLE</u>, and soared way up there.

Then Fuzzy Wuzzy became a <u>COLT</u>, a great white stallion.

And then… Fuzzy Wuzzy… became a **great, great, great, great**

<u>GREEN BAY PACKER."</u>

. . . .

When I first moved to Chicago I got a job working for the huge, downtown, department store, Marshall Field and

Company. Each morning I took a State Street bus from the Near North Side, tried to get through the side door (under the big Marshall Field clock at State and Randolph), and punch my time card by 9:00 A.M. This was difficult for <u>me</u> because I stayed out <u>late</u> at night. There is an old song, "I used to work in Chicago, in a department store." Well, I did! And, I hated it! I wonder how many people have had the same problem when they were young… lots, I'll bet! I did not want to be there so I fought with myself all along the way. To make matters worse, I worked in a dress department with a bunch of women who were well-over 40 years of age. (I was 21) They were horrible… vicious, unmannerly, and they worked on <u>commission</u>; a ruthless and bloodthirsty lot! I felt as though I took my life in my hands when I went to work. If I made more sales than they did in <u>one</u> day, they went "nuts," were envious, and made life <u>hell</u> for me. When I think about it now, they were probably more envious of my youth than the sales, but I didn't understand this at the time. I never once thought to ask for a transfer to another department where I would be happier. In those days, I was afraid of the establishment and thought, in whatever job I was laboring, I had to do exactly as I was told.

After six months, I finally mustered enough courage to quit! I landed a job at the Domino Lounge, 57 E. Walton, on the Gold Coast of Chicago's Near North Side. (Bloomingdale's is there now!) I was paid $90.weekly ($15. per night) plus tips. The tips were generous and as a result, I did well financially, and for safety, I lived at the McCormick YWCA on Oak at Dearborn. I had off on Sunday night, but worked from 8:00 P.M. in the evening until 4:00 A.M. in the morning during the rest of the week. Saturday night, we stayed open until 5:00 A.M. (Sunday). These were the hours of operation for most of the clubs and liquor licenses in the downtown Chicago area. If one had <u>not</u> <u>enough</u> to drink by 4:00 A.M. and wanted another drink, one had to find a place which stayed open all night, so, one made the trip to Cicero, a suburb of Chicago, where the saloons are open 24 hours a day. Cicero bars were supposed to close for one hour for clean-up, but the patrons usually did not leave during clean-up time. After their working hours, many folks who worked in Chicago bars headed to Cicero before going home, to enjoy a few hours of drinking and relaxation.

The Domino Lounge offered a fun and exciting time for

me. I liked to dress up, and the owners wanted me to look as glamorous as possible. Our "well-to-do" patrons were attired in expensive, gorgeous clothing, mostly evening attire. I felt I was really in the <u>heart</u> of what was happening. Chicago nightlife is great! Chicago's heartbeat can almost be felt when one walks on the sidewalks. The lounge was down the street from the Playboy Club on Walton Street, near Michigan Avenue, and a block away, on Rush Street, were night spots, like Mister Kelly's (now Gibson's), Gus' Pub (now The Whiskey), and of course, Pat Harran's, a friendly Irish pub (now Jilly's), where the young, in-crowd, liked to hang out. In the summer of 1963 there was a headliner starting to make her way into the limelight, and she was featured at Mr. Kelly's. She had a hit song called "<u>People</u>," and that was the song most frequently heard on the jukeboxes in the bars along Rush Street. That's correct! Barbra Streisand was featured at Mr. Kelly's for about a month that summer, and I think she was held over by popular demand. I never got to see her because I had to work the same hours she performed, but I always wanted to. Also, the U.S. Presidential campaigns were running fast and furiously. A team of Young Republicans was busy in the pubs each evening, touting Barry Goldwater for President. I remember this because the following November (1964) I was 23 years old, and it was my <u>first</u> opportunity, being of age, to vote in a presidential election... Lyndon B. Johnson won.

I was stuck at my job in Chicago, and missed going to Green Bay for the games and fun. Paul Hornung called me once during this time, just to say "Hi." I believe I had written to him, and that's probably how he knew where to reach me at the YWCA. (*Hi, yourself! Ask me out, Goldilocks*!).

I met Fred (Fuzzy) Thurston for the first time, at Jesse's apartment upstairs from the King's X. He had stopped there looking for someone, but I don't remember who the person was. What I do remember is... Fuzzy <u>scared</u> me... not that he made a pass at me or anything like it... but he seemed to me, to be wily and unpredictable, and I was cautious of him! What did I know? Little did I realize that as the years passed, I would grow to <u>love</u> and respect this person because of his <u>great</u> heart. In essence, I see **in** Fuzzy what I believe to be great in the human spirit... inner strength, courage and tenacity. Fuzzy never gives

195

up. I also admire Winston Churchill for some of the same reasons, and I think if they had ever met… Winston and Fuzzy would have been good buddies. Did you know "Old Winnie" gave one of the shortest but best speeches of all time, at a commencement ceremony at Cambridge University. He walked in with a big, fat cigar in his mouth… he wore a top hat and carried a cane. As he ascended to the podium, the crowd rose up to cheer him. Then, he took off the top hat, took the cigar out of his mouth, lifted the cane, and rested them on the podium. He waited… and then he said, "Never give up!" The crowd became so still one could hear a pin drop. Then, the little guy rose up on his tip-toes and said loudly, **<u>NEVER-GIVE-UP!</u>**" …he was finished with the speech. Only six words, but to me that's what it's all about… <u>never giving up</u>! It took me years before I recognized this trait in Fuzzy Thurston, and it occurred only after I had matured, and Fuzzy had survived throat cancer and financial problems, serving as an example to anyone who cares to notice… <u>Fuzzy never gives up</u>!

As I mentioned, I didn't always feel this way about Fuzzy. In the year I worked at the Domino Lounge, I asked the Packers

<u>not</u> to bring Fuzzy into the Domino when they were in town.
He sometimes had the unpredictable and uncontrollable habit
of standing on barstools, and singing at the top of his lungs.
If my boss were to get upset with me because of Fuzzy, I was
afraid I would lose my job and… I probably would have! I had
been given <u>three</u> chances to keep this job, and I <u>wanted</u> the job.
The rules were: if I missed work three times without calling
in, I was <u>not</u> to come back… I was fired! I was cautious not to
get three strikes against me, although I had already managed to
get two… and as a result, I was skating on thin ice. The owner,
Danny Miller, and his wife, Martha, were okay to work for, but
they were very strict about the operation of their business. They
wanted their establishment to cater to movie stars and to well-
known, Chicago celebrity. When the Green Bay Packers came
into the Domino Lounge the night before a game, they looked
like movie stars and they behaved like gentlemen. They were
dressed in white shirts and ties, and all wore their dark-green
Packer blazers. They were the most handsome bunch of fellows
I had ever laid eyes on. I was so proud to know them and to
think they had stopped in to see <u>me</u>. My boss was impressed I
knew them, and, it was good for his business when they came to

the lounge to say hello.

The next year, 1963, was devastating for the Packers! The proverbial writing was on the wall and, when no one came to see me (the players) at the Domino Lounge, I knew Lombardi must be "up-tight" about his team. On one, hot, August night in Soldiers Field, the Chicago Bears walloped the Packers. The pre-season loss was a sign of the season to come… the Chicago Bears dominated the league, and won the World Championship. I hated it! So did Green Bay fans… so did the Packers… and so did Vince Lombardi. To make matters worse and to fuel the rivalry between Illinois and Wisconsin, the University of Illinois went to the Rose Bowl, and won. The University of Wisconsin had gone to the Rose Bowl the year before, and lost. Talk about rubbing our noses in it!

In the spring of 1964, after I had spent about a year at the Domino, I got a call from Fuzzy Thurston. He was in town, was partying with two Chicago Bears players, and invited me to join them. How could I pass up a chance to party with them! What a thrill! I remember catching up with them at Pat Harran's saloon.

As a matter of fact, I think it was Pat who knew how to reach me and told Fuzzy. I wanted to see Fuzzy because I knew he could fill me in on Paul Hornung, since he and Paul are close friends. Well, we <u>certainly</u> had a good time! We partied for about 36 hours and at one point, at Harran's, I remember Fuzzy drank champagne out of my shoe just for the fun of it. (*Talk about a glutton for punishment!*) The first night we just couldn't stop partying at 4:00A.M., and we ended up at a bar in Cicero. I recall the owner wanted to close up and sweep the place out, but Fuzzy would not hear of it. He made all of us take brooms and mops and help the owner clean up the joint, so we wouldn't have to leave. That evening about 9:00 P.M., with no rest and totally exhausted, we ended up at one of the Chicago Bear's apartments. (I must be truthful... I was <u>exhausted</u>...and I <u>had</u> to go home to sleep... but the fellows were still strong!) Fuzzy was leaving to go back to Wisconsin, and he took me aside and began lecturing me. At first I thought he was joking, but I soon realized he was <u>dead</u> <u>serious</u>. He told me when I had lived in Wisconsin... <u>The Green Bay Packers</u> had won the World Championship, and the <u>University of Wisconsin</u> had gone the Rose Bowl. (*TRUE! So what!*) He said since I had moved to

Illinois, the <u>Chicago Bears</u> had won the World Championship, and the <u>University of Illinois</u> had gone to the Rose Bowl. His parting words were, "You bring us luck, Sandra! …Get your <u>butt</u> back to Wisconsin!"

I had not called-in to the Domino Lounge, so the next night I didn't have a job to go back to. I now had my <u>three</u> strikes against me, and I was <u>out</u>! Not sure what to do next, I stopped in to visit Tommy Downs, the restaurateur on Rush Street, and told him what had happened. He thought it was hilarious, and said there were three things I should do! First, I should go and buy myself a beautiful dress. Secondly, he would take me to dinner to the best restaurant in town. Thirdly, after dinner, he would take me to the Domino Lounge for a "Good-bye" After-Dinner drink. His logic was simple… he agreed with Fuzzy… I should go <u>home</u>… to Wisconsin.

My boss, Danny Miller, thought the <u>moon and stars</u> were hung by Tommy Downs. Tommy, a well-known, ex-Chicago policeman, had made it <u>big</u> in the restaurant business on Rush Street. Tommy had a lot of clout…and my boss respected him.

I wore the beautiful dress which Tommy had purchased for me… we went out to dinner… and then, we went for a final drink at the Domino Lounge. I thought my boss, Danny Miller, would drop his teeth when we walked in. He didn't <u>dare</u> say anything <u>ugly</u> to me although I am sure he wanted to and would have, if Tommy had not been with me. I told him this was my last night "on the town" …I was going home …and I wouldn't be coming back. I leaned over the bar and gave him a little kiss, thanking him for hiring me the year before. Then he said something absurd, and I am sure he said it because I was with Tommy Downs, and he wanted to impress him. He said any time I wanted to come back to Chicago… I could work for him. NO WAY, JOSE! Come back? All is forgiven? …I wasn't **that** dumb! And BESIDES… it was time to go home… **<u>Fuzzy had said so!</u>**

KRAMER & KRAMER (JERRY)

Jerry Seinfeld is a wealthy man and he has only **one** friend named **Kramer.** Imagine how rich I feel having **two** friends named **Kramer**! I am speaking of Jerry and Ron. These fellows are not related by blood, but they certainly have a lot in common besides their last names; they both played for Vince Lombardi, they are both true <u>INDIVIDUALS</u>, and they both <u>love</u> their Packer heritage.

. . . .

Art Currie, Dan Currie's father, was a fireman in Detroit. Naturally, he was very proud of his son who was a star of high school and college football. Being an involved and supportive father, Art Currie, kept tabs on other up-and-coming athletes around the country. He told Dan, "Keep your eyes on Idaho!" Why? Well, here's why. At the same time Dan was climbing to the top of the athletic charts at Michigan State University, Jerry Kramer was becoming a champion and making a name for himself at the University of Idaho. Little did they know they would both be drafted to Green Bay in 1958, become teammates and lifelong friends. (Here's a bit of trivia which could get you some attention. In 1958, there were four players drafted by Green Bay. Two of the four are in the Professional Football HALL OF FAME, and all of them are in the Green Bay Packer Hall of Fame. Their names are Dan Currie, Jerry Kramer, Ray Nitschke (HOF) and Jim Taylor (HOF). That is considered to be one heck of a great haul in an NFL draft. It is also interesting to note that these players, and many other greats, were already in Green Bay when Vince Lombardi came to town. The 1957 draft gave the Green Bay Packers, Paul Hornung of Notre Dame, the Heisman Trophy winner, and the legendary Ron Kramer of Michigan. Lombardi was handed a wealth of talent to work with, and to mold into the team he envisioned as his ... **WINNING TEAM!**)

Julia Roberts, the famous movie star, made a film a few years ago entitled, "Runaway Bride." I am sure <u>all</u> of the ladies saw it… maybe <u>some</u> of the men saw it, too. Anyhow, in the movie, Julia is engaged to the hometown, high-school football coach (played by Christopher Meloni of TV's <u>Law and Order - SVU</u>). The coach knows she is knowledgeable about sports trivia, and he relies on <u>her</u> to feed him names and information about sports when he cannot remember. At their engagement party, she is outside talking to Richard Gere and just when the scene starts to get "gooey" with Richard… her future groom (the coach) comes out looking for her. Under his breath he asks her what is the name of the <u>right guard</u> who played for the Green Bay Packers under Vince Lombardi? …Julia continues to make "goo-goo" eyes at Richard Gere. I start hollering at the coach, *"I know! I know! …Ask me!"* He can't hear me, so he doesn't ask me…but as Julia Roberts turns and walks away from Richard Gere, she <u>quietly</u> says to her fiancée, **"<u>Jerry Kramer.</u>"**

(I knew that!) Now…so does Christopher Meloni … so does Julia Roberts… and so does Richard Gere. And so do <u>you</u>! And don't <u>ever</u> forget it!

Jerry is the type of friend who was interested in my future before I was. When I was young he <u>always</u> encouraged me to go to college, and his prodding helped me to get it done. (*Thank you, Jerry.*) I saw him recently, and told him I am completing my Master's Degree in Business Administration. He seems as pleased as I am about my accomplishment. That's the way Jerry is… he's pleased for you and is delighted with the accomplishments of others, as well as his own. Rightly so!

When I moved back to Wisconsin from Chicago in the 1960's, I decided I wanted to go to college, this time <u>for-real</u>. I had several <u>false-starts</u> because I liked to party too much, and always dropped out. My father was becoming frustrated with my attempts at college and subsequent failures, and told me if I really wanted to go, I could prove it to him by attending the local Teachers College in a nearby community. It was <u>then</u> that I had my one-and-only, spoiled-rotten fit! I wanted to go to a **<u>big</u>** school… after all, I thought I was a **<u>big</u>** deal! (*Kids*!!!) This time however, my father would not budge, pay another lost tuition, or give me my own way. After all, I had tried college

206

about 6 or 7 times and he had a right to be disappointed in me. When I think about it now, I can't believe he was so patient with me. If it were <u>my</u> kid pulling this, I would have kicked her butt. However, my father was steadfast in his decision so, grudgingly, I registered at our County's Teachers College. I had the wanderlust so bad that when the Milwaukee Railroad's Super Locomotive, The Hiawatha, blew its whistle and passed through the little town, I held on to the desk for dear life. Man! How I wanted to be on the <u>fast</u> <u>train</u> which could take me back to the excitement of the big city of Chicago. Forget what Fuzzy had told me about returning home! What did <u>he</u> know? This was tough duty! A good friend of mine who had just divorced, and had a little boy to care for on her own, was also attending the County College. If it had not been for her, I would have bolted. She kept telling me I needed to stay, if for no other reason than to help <u>her</u> get through. So I stayed! …and, I said it was to help her, but in truth, I was having some success and was finally finishing a <u>whole</u> semester without dropping out. Of course, I had a lot of help… it wasn't all my doing… my success was a combination of my friend's, my parent's, and the faculty's <u>help</u>, which by sheer good luck was there to support me. Support is so <u>vital</u> to success, and I realized I was in the <u>right</u> place at the right time. I was really <u>proud</u> of this accomplishment. It was a start! I stayed there for Spring Semester, <u>only</u>. ... I had proved <u>myself</u> to my father, and when the semester was finished, my friend and I, along with her little boy, went to Stevens Point to Summer School at the Wisconsin State Teacher's College. My Dad fixed up a big, green, 4-door, 1958 Studebaker for us to drive back and forth. It had belonged to my Uncle Frank who had died a few days after Kennedy was assassinated. It had about 2,000 miles on the odometer, and had been in storage in a building on our land. It wasn't "COOL" by my standards, but the darn thing was a classic beauty and it weighed a <u>ton</u>, so my dad was sure we would be safe, and in the event we hit a deer, we had a fighting chance of survival. In the fall of 1964, I stayed in Stevens Point to continue college, working toward my degree, and my friend and her little boy went back home... and I really missed them.

During the Spring Semester, while I was still attending the local County College and living at home with my parents, the State of Wisconsin offered its first Turkey Hunt. A few years before, The Department of Natural Resources had planted a bunch of turkeys just north of my home, and the flock had grown large enough in numbers to warrant a hunting season. The only way one could get a license was to enter a lottery. Jerry Kramer loves to hunt, so he took a chance on the Turkey Hunting Lottery and <u>won</u> a license to hunt the "little buggers." I couldn't believe he won… I thought the State had given him some special privilege because he played for the Green Bay Packers. Of course, they had not! Jerry won because he had bought a ticket. Anyhow, because of this happening, I learned one of life's greatest lessons, and I will share it with you now. The lesson is: IF YOU WANT TO WIN THE LOTTERY, YOU HAVE TO BUY A TICKET! …Or in other words, you cannot expect any rewards in life if you are not willing to pay the price and participate… you have to be **in** to <u>win</u>!!!

One spring day during the Turkey Hunt, Jerry Kramer arrived at my house with his friend, Art Laha. Art was a famous man in his own right. He was a sportsman who had been written up several times in Field and Stream magazine. He owned and operated a hunting camp at Winchester, WI and he was a famous World Class Archery Champion. At the time, it was legal to hunt polar bears, and I believe Art Laha is the only man to have killed a Polar bear with a bow and arrow. At least he held that record at the time of their visit. Just in case you are wondering…hunting, let alone, <u>killing</u> a polar bear with a bow and arrow is not an easy thing to do! In later years I had a man work for me who mowed my lawn, and I told him about this visit of Jerry Kramer and Art Laha. The man got really excited! I thought he was interested in knowing about Jerry, but he wanted to know about Art. He asked me to show him <u>exactly</u> where Art Laha had walked, so he could walk in his footsteps. I had no idea that Art was such a revered sportsman. Art had a film about Alaska, and part of the way he earned his livelihood was showing films of his hunting adventures. As he showed the films, he recited Robert W. Service's poetry. I will never forget the "goose-pimples" I got on my arms when Art… a very, dramatic showman, recited from Service's poem, "The Spell of the Yukon":

> There's a land where the mountains are nameless,
>> And the rivers all run God knows where;
>> There are lives that are erring and aimless,

And deaths that just hang by a hair;

There are hardships that nobody reckons;

There are valleys unpeopled and still;

There's a land - oh, it beckons and beckons,

And I want to go back - and <u>I will</u>.

When 35 years later, I received the opportunity to go to
Alaska, I went. I made it a point to tell Jerry the moment I knew
I was going. As usual, he was pleased for me. He had always
told me I would fall in love with Alaska, and would not want to
return home... and he was correct!

Back to the story-

Art and Jerry were both dressed in buckskins, fringe and
all, and they looked like real frontiersmen; as though they
had just stepped out of the 18th century, and Art, being part
Native American and French Canadian by birth, fit the role of
frontiersman even more so than Jerry. He had a bear skin rug
with him which he and Jerry laid over the double bed in our
guest room. They wanted my parents and me to realize the size

211

of a Brown bear, and it was so huge it enveloped the entire bed, and hung well-over the sides. I had no idea until that day, what people mean when they say a bear can get <u>big</u>! Really BIG!

The afternoon had been very wet and rainy, so they had stopped hunting early. My mother fixed the fellows a little lunch. Jerry gave her a big hug in thanks for the lunch and quipped, "Ollie, I wonder where the turkeys go when it <u>rains</u>?" My mom was a farm girl and a great "one-liner." She said, "They go under the <u>porch</u>." Jerry and Art cracked up!

A few years ago, Jerry was named the CEO of a worldwide networking company. On one of the first conference calls which announced Jerry as the new CEO, he told about growing up in Idaho. He reminded hundreds of listeners of some of the great lessons he had learned from Coach Lombardi. He told a worldwide audience how a few years back, he (Jerry) had run into financial difficulties, and as a result had to sell some of his beloved, Idaho ranch on the Snake River. Initially, he thought he could settle and be satisfied with the realization he still retained about 60 acres of his property. Jerry had tried to come to terms with the fact he was now a "60 acre" fellow. He couldn't! He knew he was a "600 and even a 6,000 acre" man. I agree with him… I know him, and he is definitely not a "60 acre" man. He is a <u>big</u> man and a <u>big</u> thinker… he entertains <u>big</u> dreams! There would be no way <u>Jerry Kramer</u> would settle for less than what he is worth, especially to himself. I believe all of us should think about this. Some people never think they are worth, or worthy of greatness and a big paycheck, so they settle for far less than what they are truly worth. The famous insurance guru, W. Clement Stone, printed a motivational poem with the line "anything I had asked of life, life would have willingly paid." Jerry works hard and pays himself what he thinks he's worth, and rightly so. I respect him for this, and I appreciate and follow his example. Jerry is a Champion… and I believe he was instrumental in helping me believe that I have what it takes to be a Champion, too. Do you know… each of us can be a Champion if we believe we can?

Through the early Packer years Jerry had a few injuries, but mostly the normal, run-of-the-mill football injuries, which can be expected when one plays professional football for a living.

Then he got sick, and I mean… **really** sick. No one knew what was wrong with him. He started getting thinner and thinner, until finally alarmed, Lombardi sent him to Mayo Clinic to be examined and where he was immediately hospitalized. Jerry was dying and no one could figure out why. They did all sorts of tests. They did an exploratory operation and a bowel dissection. Of course they did not have today's knowledge of medicine and technology to locate the source of an ailment. For several weeks, Jerry lay near death and I recall hearing that someone had to stay next to him to turn his body every little while. The testing continued, and finally physicians discovered something which was not supposed to be in Jerry's body. Operating again, surgeons pulled out a splinter which was embedded in his back side, lower quadrant. How did it get there? Well… when Jerry was a teen (1953) in Idaho, working on the ranch, he was gathering cattle into a shelter to help protect them from an incoming storm. The temperature had dropped to well below zero and when one of the steer stepped on a frozen plank in the barnyard, the impact of the hoof on the rock-solid wood, shot slivers into Jerry's back. At the time he was rushed to Spokane, WA where a 7.5 inch splinter, as big around as his thumb, was removed from the large muscle in his back, and the physicians thought they had removed <u>everything</u>. Eleven years later (1964) at Mayo Clinic, a puncture was discovered in his large intestine, and a tumor was found in his liver. As they searched for the source of the ailment, they found the other wood splinter. Ironically, <u>wood</u> is the same <u>density</u> as <u>human tissue,</u> so the splinter did <u>not</u> show up on an x-ray. Once the splinter was removed, Jerry readily regained his health.

What a fortunate man… a "6,000 acre" man and <u>worth</u> every acre! Personally, I too feel fortunate that he lived because my achievements would be fewer, and my life would be <u>less</u> interesting… if I had never met… Jerry Kramer.

Right Guard, Jerry Kramer sits next to #66 (Ray Nitschke) on the bench during a game in 1968. From the collection of Vernon Biever (copyright)

I snapped this picture of Jerry Kramer in Lambeau Field in
September 1970. It was the first time I got to sit on the bench during
the game. Notice the height of the stadium wall in the background
compared to now.

(From left to right) Dan Currie, the author, and Jerry Kramer. Three
old friends still having fun together. Alumni weekend, October-1998.
Photo by Nick Martone, Las Vegas, NV

Jerry Kramer rests his arm on me while he tells a funny story in the
back room of Fuzzy's. October-1998.
Photo by Nick Martone, Las Vegas, NV

Ron Kramer is forced down by a Detroit Lion player. Circa 1962.
From the collection of Vernon Biever (copyright)

Vince Lombardi and Ron Kramer convey their mutual respect. Photo from a Detroit Free Press publication and from the private collection of Ron Kramer with permission.

A big hug from my dear friend, Ron Kramer. Green Bay, December-1998. From the Author's collection

KRAMER & KRAMER (RON)

There is a lot of wonderful information about Ron Kramer that I will not tell… the book would be too long. Here is the good stuff which I can share. First of all, some of us playfully refer to him as Mr. Right but more about that, later!

Ron scared the heck out of me when I was young. He is a tough guy and he always seemed to be growling. As I have come to know him better through the years, I must say he is the sort of fellow you never want to have for an enemy. If you challenge him, he will try to beat you at any game you want to play. He always plays to <u>win</u>, and he will <u>never</u> give an inch. He can be ruthless and without remorse or pity. It is very important to understand <u>he doesn't care</u> at all what others think of him.

Therefore, he has nothing to lose. But on the same token, if he is your friend and you are his friend, he will protect you, fight for you, and would maybe die for you, if necessary. When <u>he</u> considers you his <u>friend</u>, you can not be more <u>blessed</u>.

I refer to Ron as a person with a "D" personality. You will understand what I mean when I describe him to you. Ron Kramer is <u>D</u>etermined, <u>D</u>efining, <u>D</u>eliberate, <u>D</u>emanding, <u>D</u>ogmatic, <u>D</u>omineering, <u>D</u>iscriminating and <u>D</u>ictatorial. Get the picture? In other words, he's a man who knows what he wants and usually, gets it! He uses these characteristics to accomplish whatever task he undertakes. A friend of mine tells me when Ron played football at Michigan, it seemed as though there was no one else on the team…he was the whole team. Please indulge me when I say I think of him as being like a male mountain goat on a narrow mountain path who encounters another male mountain goat… and they butt heads. In this circumstance, the path is <u>too</u> narrow for either of them to pass without <u>one</u> falling to his death …so which one wins? Well, in the case of the mountain goats, the older more dominant male wins. The younger animal gets down and allows the older male to cross over him, walking on his back. In Ron's case, he is usually the dominant male for whom the lesser backs down. He is usually <u>right</u> and commands the respect of others. Don't misunderstand me… if Ron Kramer knows he is wrong, or is <u>not</u> the one with the most power, he <u>readily</u> accepts it and humbly assumes a position which will allow someone to walk over him. That takes a <u>big</u> man and he is fair about it, but due to Ron's nature… it does not happen very often.

It is said, Ron Kramer is probably the first tight end in the NFL. Some may disagree because the official determination is not <u>clear</u>. However, when Ron was drafted along with Paul Hornung in 1957, the name "Tight End" was not used to describe any position on the team. Ron was a superior athlete; big, fast, and smart. He knew the running and passing game; could reverse sides and go either way… and he could tackle. In other words, here was a player who because of his ability, created a <u>new</u> position which would become very important to the game. It would seem as though Ron had filled a need. In specific terms, he was the weak-side end on an unbalanced line. As the position developed, it became known as the <u>tight end</u>

position. Intelligent Ron Kramer was everywhere he needed to be on offense; a pioneer of the position.

Kramer is a graduate of the University of Michigan and is one of five athletes to have had their numbers retired at that school. One of those five became President of the United States, Gerald Ford, and you can bet they did <u>not</u> retire Ford's number because of his <u>athletic</u> ability. Ron lettered in Football, Basketball, and Track. If Ron had decided to become a professional basketball player, he could have chosen to be one. In fact he thought about it, but he broke his leg in his first season at Green Bay and decided to stay with football once the leg mended.

Ron tells wonderful stories about what it was like in the <u>old</u> days in Green Bay. He says when he came to Green Bay in 1957 the stadium at the University of Michigan was three times larger than the Packer's stadium. As a matter of record, it is <u>still</u> larger… seating over 110,000, and Lambeau Field, even after its recent renovation, can <u>still</u> only accommodate about 72,000 by comparison. He also comments that after his <u>college</u> glory years, the attention which was given him in pro-football at Green Bay was somewhat quiet and subdued. In other words, he is a college legend: the legendary Ron Kramer of Michigan

In 1957, Ron became friends with Max McGee and Paul Hornung and they rented a house together. They had a great deal of fun and when you ask Ron if the stories about McGee and Hornung are true, he will tell you if you multiply that number by a thousand, you may be closer to reality. I first met Ron when he lived with Max and Paul in their little house near downtown Green Bay. Paul brought me over and introduced me to him. Ron just stood there and stared at me. He did not say a word…not one word. He just stared. I was really intimated and of course, that's what he was trying to do…intimidate me. He succeeded. He is an intimidating fellow, and I did not know at the time that years later he would become a fan of **me** and would help me, not only with business but also with friendship. And what a fan to have on my side, cheering for me! When my father died I received three calls from Ron who was "just checking" to make sure I was doing okay. I was devastated by the death, and even though my father was an old man, Ron was kind, consoling, and understanding, saying all the right things to comfort me. I told Ron I was feeling, for the first time in my life, all <u>alone</u>. "Well, hey, kid," he said sympathetically, "you've still got **us**." He was trying to make me feel better and after I thought about it awhile, I <u>really</u> felt terrible. If <u>they</u> are all I have left… wow…I <u>really</u> am in trouble. Just kidding! Ron, in his kindness, was telling me I still have good friends among the Lombardi Packers, especially in him. Thank you, big guy! You are a prize! But definitely, a <u>consolation</u> prize!

Kramer has a great attitude about life… he is **<u>always</u>** positive and I really like that in a person. He was the head of a big steel company in Detroit which went down the tubes when the bottom fell out of the steel market in 1981. Though he lost a fortune, it did <u>not</u> get the better of him. He kept right on truckin' because he has a good, positive, mental attitude. To me, attitude is the key to everything! Your attitude determines your altitude, and you can never reach <u>high</u> places without having a positive attitude. You can never pull yourself up out of a hole without it. You can't get anywhere without it. It is the catalyst which propels you onward and upward. Ron's parents were instrumental in instilling this in him. When Ron's company failed, he went to his father and told him he had lost… it had gone under. His father listened and then he assured Ron that <u>he</u> had <u>not</u> gone under…only the company had. Ron was just "back to <u>even</u>." This reminds me of my father who always told me the only endeavor at which one can start at the <u>top</u> is <u>digging a hole</u>. In addition, Ron's family provided him with never-ending support. He will tell you it doesn't matter how much talent someone has, it will probably never be fully realized without the support of family and/or those who care. Ron's mother went to every event in which he participated. When his father died, his mother was 62 years old, and though she had never driven a car, she was determined to get to all the games. She took driving lessons and got her license, and she attended 281 straight games to give Ron the support he needed. Paul Hornung's mother was the same way, and she dedicated her life to giving Paul the support and confidence he needed, not to mention her help in the development of his fantastic personality. If you want to know some of the things that mothers do for their sons, check the Preface of this book.

Ron is a loving and sentimental fellow who cares about his family and his relationships. He is extremely loyal and that is why I say, if he counts you as a friend, you are indeed fortunate. When Ron was playing at Green Bay, his little boy, Kurt, lost an eye when a shoe lace snapped up and hit him. Ron realized he had to be nearer to his son. He had a good relationship with Vince Lombardi, and after playing out his option, he left the Green Bay Packers to be closer to his family. Lombardi had respect for Ron's integrity as a family man and he let him leave with no hard feelings. Obviously, Ron Kramer had his priorities in order, and for Ron, his family has priority over the Green Bay Packers.

With his priorities in order, Ron left Green Bay in 1964 just before the big winning streak that would make the Lombardi Packers the legends they are today, and before the inception of something that would become part of our American Culture… The Super Bowl. I have heard that Lombardi regretted saying …"winning isn't everything … it's the only thing." He wanted to add more to these thoughts and include the ordered-priorities of God, Family, Country… and Vocation. I have placed a picture in this book which portrays the respect shared by Kramer and Lombardi. Ron is wearing a <u>Detroit Lion</u> uniform, and he and Vince are respectfully looking each other in the eyes, and shaking hands. The picture tells the whole story.

A few years back at Christmastime, I arranged an autograph-signing trip which took Willie Wood, Boyd Dowler, Ron Kramer, Fuzzy Thurston, and me around the State of Wisconsin visiting several of the hotels and casinos. We had a lot of laughs and were <u>often</u> entertained by Ron's navigational skills, getting us from one place to another. No matter which way one of us decided to travel, Kramer had a <u>faster and better</u> way. There was head-butting but Kramer <u>always</u> overruled and we let him walk all over us. Gee! I have no idea how we would have made it if it had not been for "Mr. Right" leading the way.

I love one <u>particular</u> story that Ron tells. When playing at the University of Michigan he looked forward to the weekly visit of an old man who would bring apples on Wednesday afternoons to autumn football practice. Ron says the man became known as "Mr. Apple." The man would bring a bushel of wonderful-tasting apples and set them out for the players to enjoy. In these present years, Ron carries on the tradition, and now it is <u>he</u> who brings the apples for the team. One day he overheard one of the young players ask another, "Hey! Who is the ***old guy*** who brings us the apples?" Well, what can I say? That's life! …But, you can be sure it is someone like Ron Kramer who takes the time to continue to do a good thing, and to do it "right." Come to think of it …he is always "right!" He is "Mr. Right."

PAUL HORNUNG MARRIES

Finally entrenched at college, I was having a great year...
and discovered I was an actress... so I joined the Drama
Department and won the Best Supporting Actress and the
Best Actress awards ...plus, I got good grades. Bound and
determined to stay in college, I was not going to get side-
tracked by going over to Green Bay, and not returning to school
on Monday mornings. Once I got the hang of it, I scheduled all
of my classes to fit my party schedule, and never signed up for
classes on Tuesdays. This left me <u>free</u> to party on Monday night
in Green Bay, or Appleton, with the team.

Staying in Green Bay with the fans after a game is a lot
of fun, but Monday night with the players is even more fun.

On Monday night we stayed home and watched "Rowan and Martin's Laugh-In" and then around 9:00 or 9:30 P.M. we met at Fuzzy's Left Guard in Appleton, and shared the laughs which Goldie Hawn and others had provided on the show. Donny Anderson (Green Bay Packers 1966- 1970) was a friend and player, who shared these laughs and a few cocktails with me on these evenings. We would try to remember all the funny lines from the show, and we had so much fun, no one could blame a person for not wanting to return to work or to school, the next day. But, I <u>always</u> made it back for class by <u>Wednesday</u>.

During my first semester I got a couple of calls from Jerry Kramer saying he was proud of me, but he cautioned me <u>not</u> to leave Stevens Point until I got the hang of school. "Stay there now… you have a good start. Don't screw it up!" When I graduated from college, I sent all the Packers who would appreciate my accomplishment a graduation announcement, just to let them know I made it.

It was during one of these first semesters, I received the terrible news that Paul Hornung was getting married… (*I wanted to die*)… and to a centerfold… <u>Darn it</u>! I was crushed… my hero was being captured… how could I go on? And, he was sooo cute! What made it worse is… I had always wanted to know what he wanted me to do when we made love. He <u>promised</u> he would tell me, but he never did. Then this "bunny" shows up from out of nowhere, and I'm told the reason he is marrying her is because she poured champagne all over him and licked it off. Why didn't he tell me that's what he wanted? I could have done that… I <u>like</u> champagne! Ron Kramer said Paul did it to <u>him</u>… and it was great! I hope he was joking!

The wedding took place at the cathedral in Santa Monica, CA and of course, I wasn't invited, but a lot of my friends were, and Dan Currie and Fuzzy Thurston were ushers. Dan says the (bunny) bride really wanted to get married in Hawaii… that she entertained an exotic dream about being married someplace over there. Dan told her it was <u>good</u> of her not to insist that the ceremony be in Hawaii, and praised her saying, at least she was considerate enough to have the ceremony on <u>this</u> Continent… making it possible for some of <u>Paul</u>'s friends to attend. Jerry West, the basketball player, was a guest, and I thought it was great to have a famous, big-name, basketball player there with the Green Bay Packers, and for Paul.

There was a movie star named Gilbert Roland sitting inside the cathedral and Dan poked Fuzzy and said, "Is <u>that</u> who I think it is?" Fuzzy nodded and said, "Yeah, I think it **is**." Gilbert Roland was a handsome, old-time, movie star with a magnificent charm about him… perhaps you remember him. After the ceremony, Dan went over to speak with him and inquired if he was a guest at the wedding. Mr. Roland asked, "Whose wedding?" Dan told him Paul Hornung was getting married, and Mr. Roland said, "No," he was <u>not</u> a guest. He told Dan he had stopped into the church to say a prayer, and had no idea one of <u>his</u> **"heroes"** was getting married. That's really a nice story, isn't it? See, Paul! I'm not the <u>only</u> one… who considers you their <u>hero</u>!

OTHER GOLDEN BOYS

Heart to Hart

Being around and knowing most of the Green Bay Packers in the 1960's, when Lombardi was coaching, was an exciting time. Many of the players were unique unto themselves, and it seemed as though these individuals were there because destiny had somehow, delivered them to Green Bay. One of these special players is a fellow by the name of Doug Hart. Doug is a talented, intelligent man, with a wonderful personality, who had earned his way to primary starter at right cornerback by 1964. He was a real student of football and involved himself in the intensity of Lombardi's coaching. He also loved to hunt and fish, and had a pilot's license and plane. In those years he could be found flying around Austin-Streubel Field most any time he was <u>not</u> practicing and playing football, or hunting and fishing.

One day I was returning to Steven Point, WI where I was attending college, and my flight had a layover in Green Bay. I would be required to wait for a couple of hours, and change planes in order to get to my destination. To kill time, I wandered around the airport and finally went into the coffee shop to get something to eat. Doug was in the restaurant and I was pleased to see his familiar smiling face. When I told him about my wait, he offered to fly me to Stevens Point, and I jumped at the chance to spend time with him, and to fly in his private plane. It was winter, and snow covered the ground in patches, making it look like a black and white checkerboard. Every time we moved over a snow-covered patch of ground onto a blackened area, the small plane jolted and the turbulence frightened me, until Doug explained that the sun's reflection off the black and white areas caused a change in energy and radiation waves, further causing the small plane to jump as we passed through them. Because of his logical explanation, I have never again been frightened when a plane encounters turbulence. (*Thanks, Doug!*)

On several occasions during the off-season, Doug would come to Stevens Point on business, and I could <u>always</u> depend on an invitation from him for a few cocktails and dinner at the Hot Fish Shop, a popular downtown restaurant. He was delightful company and I needed this kind of entertainment on occasion to assure my remaining in a small college town. He encouraged my endeavors in school, and also advised me on business ventures which I was pursuing.

Doug was happily married, so I never misconstrued the invitations for cocktails and dinner as a date, and we were always accompanied by business associates from the area. I think Doug realized however, that it was important for me to have <u>another</u> life besides school, and I think he enjoyed my presence… as we shared a lot of laughs. One evening, Doug gave me a ride home to the house I shared with other college students. Someone had broken beer bottles in the driveway, and the broken glass punctured every tire on his beautiful automobile. I felt awful, and there wasn't much I could do about it, but he probably thought I was a <u>risky</u> person to ask out.

Doug's business savvy would cause him to become a prominent businessman, and he was made President of a company out of Minneapolis which was the world's largest producer of portable toilets. He also became a Vice-President of Artic Cat, in charge of corporate development; the company which makes snowmobiles. I know he never lost his enthusiasm for adventure and for hunting and fishing because, although he is semi-retired and living in Florida, he is a Coast Guard Captain and a fly-fishing instructor. Some people, like Doug, pack a lot of living into their life.

Recently, as I passed a group of people at a Packer Alumni banquet in Green Bay, someone in the crowd called out after me. "SANDY!" When I turned to learn who had called my name, I was delighted to see the joy-filled, ever-smiling face of my friend, Doug Hart.

THE GOLD DUST TWINS

(Grabo and Donny)

When Vince Lombardi came to Green Bay he found a team already assembled there, and it was his task to re-arrange the personnel into a unit which could win ballgames. This he did with great ability and we know the outcome. As time went on key players like Paul Hornung left, requiring Lombardi to recruit college and other athletes, as replacements.

In 1966, Vince Lombardi added two college athletes to the Green Bay roster; Jim Grabowski of the University of Illinois and Donny Anderson of Texas Tech University, and the deal involved over $1,000,000 to acquire them. Because of this record amount of money, the two <u>soon</u> became known as the Gold Dust Twins. I didn't meet Jim Grabowski until years later, when I booked both he and Donny into an autograph-signing session. When I met him I liked him right away, and because he is a friend of Donny, he had my attention from the get-go. In present years I can say both <u>he</u> and Donny are my friends.

241

I love the story Donny tells… of when Lombardi recruited him for the "big bucks." As I said, such a large amount of money had <u>never</u> <u>before</u> been rendered to get a couple of rookies, and when the deal was made, Donny lit up a big, fat cigar, and several pictures appeared of him with the cigar in his mouth and a big grin on his face. Shortly thereafter, a picture appeared in the newspaper of Fuzzy Thurston with other Packer players, and Fuzzy also had a big, fat cigar stuck between his teeth and was sporting a big grin. Lombardi asked Fuzzy, "Why the <u>cigar</u> … all of a sudden?" Fuzzy replied, "Well, I see the rookie has one, and from what I hear… <u>he's doing okay$</u>!"

One time I got such a kick out of Jim Grabowski when he stopped at Fuzzy's during an Alumni weekend. He said he tried to go by the saloon without stopping, but his car stopped automatically. He said he had no control, and could <u>not</u> make it by without stopping to see who was there. I feel the same way, and I'll bet once <u>you</u> visit Fuzzy's, you will, too! I'll probably see you there!

I had a great, big crush on Donny Anderson, but I never let him know. (*I'm sure he guessed*). He was single and a great catch, but in those days, if a fellow was four years younger than a girl it was like robbing the cradle. I wish I had known then, that when women get older, younger men are ideal companions. Donny was four years younger than me and I considered that to give me <u>seniority</u>…like he was <u>still</u> in 8th grade and I was a <u>big-shot</u> senior in High School. How foolish! (*Four years?*)

Donny and I looked forward to seeing each other at Fuzzy's on Monday nights. (Incidentally, there was <u>no</u> Monday Night Football then!) I used to dress up, <u>especially</u>, so Donny would comment on the way I looked. One time he told me… I looked just like a movie star. WOW! What a compliment from such a gorgeous guy, but we never dated.

At the end of the 1968 season, I met Donny at Fuzzy's on the last Monday night we would ever spend there. I remember he had just purchased a beautiful Paul Peugeot (gold and diamond) wristwatch and I was admiring it. He said he was leaving the next morning to go back to Texas. I was graduating from college in the spring, and I figured I would never see him again. I said I wanted to <u>kiss</u> him **good-bye**, and Donny said, as much as he would like that kiss, he didn't think it was a very, good idea because he had the flu. I didn't care… so… I kissed him. … I mean …I <u>really</u> kissed him! I spent the next month in bed, not with Donny, unfortunately, but… with the flu.

I painted this picture of Boyd Dowler from a little photograph while
I was in college. (1968) When I took it to Green Bay to give to him,
someone stole it from my room.

Million dollar hero, Donny Anderson #44, earning his money as Gale Gillingham clears the way. From the collection of Vernon Biever (copyright)

A picture of two people who love each other. Fuzzy Thurston and Boyd Dowler in Green Bay, June -1998. Photo by the Author

MRS. FUZZY

(A WARM AND FUZZY LOVE STORY)

Sometimes, little is known about the women who are married to professional athletes, but they are the ones in the background and on the sidelines, making sure that life runs smoothly while their men are out "slaying dragons." They do so much to make their husbands great and one of these commendable women is Susan Ann Thurston, wife of Fred "Fuzzy" Thurston, and it is she… who has served as the better half, raising a family, and sticking it out through good and bad times, continually re-convincing Fuzzy that he had been right, and had picked a winner when he married her. It is well-known that Susan Ann and Fuzzy love each other very much, but this is not to say there were <u>not</u> times when she would have preferred to "wring his neck," as the saying goes, but alas, had to resign herself to the fact that this is the way it is, when you marry… a <u>Fuzzy Thurston</u>.

One of the best stories I know which gives an example of this, takes place early in the Lombardi years when Vince and Marie Lombardi gave a party, and invited the team and their wives. All the men wore their best suits, shirts and ties, and the ladies were attired in their fancy finery. Susan Ann and Fuzzy were no exception, and she had given Fuzzy several wifely warnings about how important it was, since he was all dressed up, to behave properly and conduct himself like a gentleman. After the party, many of the couples ended up at Speed's, the popular saloon in downtown Green Bay, and just before entering the building, Susan Ann once <u>again</u> reminded Fuzzy that he had better be on his best behavior…or else. (Or else what, you may ask?)

After a few cocktails and some good-natured horsing around, the band began to play loudly, and it was obvious that Fuzzy was ready to party. When Susan Ann noticed his gyrations she turned to him and emphatically, cried a warning to him… "FRED!!!" To which he replied as loudly as he could holler… "<u>That's</u> <u>right</u>, Susan Ann, take a <u>good</u> <u>look</u> at the <u>big</u> <u>ASS</u> you married!!!" (*Oh, my goodness!*)

Paul Hornung lived with Fuzzy and Susan Ann, on and off, when he played for the Packers. She has many stories which make all of us roll with laughter and she had the inside track of many situations which arose and involved Paul. One night when she was pregnant with their daughter, Tori, and was about a day from delivery… she was awakened very late by Fuzzy and Paul returning home. They were loud, and Susan Ann could also hear a woman crying. Curious about what was going on in her own home, she went downstairs to investigate, and she found Paul, Fuzzy, and a girl that Paul had brought home, in her kitchen. The girl must have had reservations about being there because she kept on wailing that her fiancée was going to kill her because they were getting married on Saturday. Finally, Susan Ann put her "foot down" and said she could not stay, and that she should leave <u>now</u>. The girl left and everyone went to bed, but about ten minutes later there was a loud banging on the front door, and everyone got up and went to see who was there. The girl who had just left, was standing by the front door and she was <u>again</u> sobbing… but this time it was because she had driven her car into a ditch. Paul and Fuzzy went out in their <u>underwear</u> to check the situation. About a block down the street, the girl's Volkswagen Bug was leaning into a deep ditch. Paul got on one side of the car and Fuzzy got on the other and they simply lifted the car out of the ditch, and placed it back on the highway. And away she went! It is very handy to have fellows like Fuzzy and Paul around, especially when you need a hand or a <u>lift</u>.

Don't ever think that Fuzzy does not know what Susan Ann has done for him though the years. When he had cancer, he says it was <u>she</u> who was the strong one, and helped him through the struggle. When he faced financial trouble, it was <u>she</u> who stood by him, and gave him the strength to go on. Ironically, when Fuzzy and Susan Ann were interviewed by a reporter about their struggle and survival, the reporter asked to interview them separately, probably to see if they had different slants on the story. When he finished the interview and read his notes, he was astounded that both had answered the questions with almost the exact <u>same</u> <u>words</u>. To me... this is one of the greatest indications that people are really <u>together</u>, communicate with one another, and are a true <u>couple</u>.

"It must have been cold there in my <u>shadow</u>," are the beginning words to the song, **<u>The Wind Beneath My Wings</u>**. (Remember, Fuzzy has no larynx and when he gets up and sings this song to Susan Ann, <u>I am the one who chokes up</u>.) I know how lucky Fuzzy is... to have <u>her</u>. I know she lifted him up. I know she was <u>content</u> to let <u>him</u> shine. When you love someone... you <u>let</u> them shine. He may have been the "one with all the <u>glory</u>" but she was the "one with all the <u>strength</u>," and because of her... he **could**... "fly higher than an eagle..." because of <u>her</u>.

Need I say more? I believe I could fill a book with stories about Fuzzy, but, if I write such a book, <u>volumes</u> will have to be written and dedicated to his <u>great</u> wife... Susan Ann.

Fuzzy in his tuxedo with his lovely wife, Susan Ann   Photo from
the private Fred Thurston Collection with permission

Fuzzy, Susan Ann and another Green Bay legend, Brett Favre. Photo from the private Fred Thurston collection with permission

Bret Favre autographed this photo for Susan Ann. "To Sue - From your favorite Packer. Too bad, Fuzzy. Love, Brett Favre" She won't part with the autographed picture so I had to use this one, sans the autograph. Photo from the private Fred Thurston collection with permission

NORTH DALLAS $FORTY

You may remember the movie, "North Dallas Forty," starring Nick Nolte and Mac Davis. It was filmed in the 1970's and I think the movie, though somewhat graphic, is fairly accurate in depicting some of the wild times which went on in those football days; the Packer days of my youth. I suppose what goes on today is even wilder. I call this chapter, "North Dallas $Forty," not because of the film, but because that's what it cost me, one, hot summer night getting to and from a Packer party in Dallas.

I was madly in love with one of the eligible Packers, and I told this fellow I was going on vacation and would be in Dallas for the Packer-Cowboy game on August 24, 1967. It was to be a <u>night</u> game, scheduled for 8:30 P.M. in the Cotton Bowl. He was delighted I was coming to see the game, and of course, he secured tickets for me right behind the Packer bench about 15 rows up. I sat next to the nephew of Lee Roy Caffey (Green Bay Packers 1964-1969). The nephew was a sweet kid, about 17 or 18 years old, who was more fascinated by me and my exploits, than he was by the game. He was fun; we shared the excitement of being there and became <u>instant</u> pals.

The trip to Dallas was jinxed! I was settled in my hotel room when the front desk called, asking me to change rooms. Apparently they had made a mistake in their bookings, so I obliged them but I shouldn't have, because in the mix-up, they forgot to change my room number at the switchboard. As a result, they lost track of me in the hotel and no calls were coming through. I knew something was wrong but couldn't figure out what had happened. I was expecting my fellow to call and make arrangements with me to meet him after the game… as he had told me he would. I wasn't used to traveling at that time in my life, and I was a bit anxious about being in Dallas on my own. It never occurred to me the fellow had not tried to call me at all, and I mistakenly blamed the absence of communication on the hotel's room mix-up. When I got to the Cotton Bowl, my player/friend waved to me as he was coming off the field. *SWOON*! It was a hot night in Dallas, and since I didn't know the plans, I hopped a cab back to my hotel to wait in the cool of my room. It got later and later and no one called. I kept checking with the switchboard to make sure they knew my location, and I became more and more anxious. I sensed something bad had happened or was about to happen. Something was not right! I was scared and wanted my Mama, but nevertheless, I was in Dallas, a long way from home, and alone. I had to make the most of it. Right? I must have checked my hair and make-up a dozen times during the wait. I was ready to leave as soon as I got the call, and finally at around 2:00 A.M. the phone rang, and I was surprised to hear Ray Nitschke's voice. He said, "Hey, kid, you're invited to a party. Get a pen and write down this address." I did, and told him I would be there soon. I assumed my fellow had asked him to call and invite me… he must have. Right? Well… I got into a taxi and traveled forever and forever, or so it seemed. About 45 minutes later we pulled into an apartment complex and stopped, and the cabbie said it would be $20 for the ride… the meter was on and racking up the many miles. When I got out of the cab, Ray Nitschke was standing at the curb, and I said, "Hi, Ray." "Hey, kid! Are <u>you</u> **sure** you want to go in there?" I said, "Sure, why <u>not</u>?" "Your choice… I'm gonna' leave." He got into another cab and pulled away. Suddenly I was scared-to-death and my stomach rolled over, but I lifted my chin and <u>bravely</u> followed the noise to a downstairs apartment, crawling with people… some of whom I knew, but a lot more I didn't. Many seemed drunk, it was extremely loud, and after wading through the crowd, I spotted Jerry Kramer in the kitchen area and pushed through so I could stand next to him. I hate going into places alone… I am sure you <u>ladies</u> know what I mean. The apartment was filled with smoke and the visibility was so poor one could barely see across the room. Next to me was a big armchair with a fellow seriously making-out with the girl sitting on his lap. In fact, many of the partygoers in the room were <u>similarly</u> occupied. It was dark and the rock and roll music was blaring. Jerry and I tried to converse but we could hardly hear each other over the noise. Paul Hornung's estranged wife, the ex-bunny, came over and started to talk with us. Wow! Great! I heard they were separated… and I had never met her, so I was really curious. She was very nice to me and really pretty! She asked me if I had dated Paul, and she smiled when I shyly said, "*Yes!*" Jerry got us each a drink and she was trying to tell me, over the noise, about this wonderful new ladies' apparel called "pantyhose," and how I would love them and should buy some. In those days, most women wore garters and nylon stockings, usually with seams up the back. Those who were really modern and bold, or lazy because we didn't want to be straightening seams all the time, bought seamless stockings. But, WOW, panty hose! What a great idea! She jokingly said the boys didn't like them because they were harder to get into, if you get her meaning. Jerry laughed, half listening to our girl-talk, watching and enjoying the crowd. When she drifted away, I started to adjust my eyes to the darkness and look around. The passionate pair in the armchair beside me uncoupled just far enough so I could see who the fellow was. Can you imagine my utter dismay (and shock) when I looked down and recognized my fellow with this girl on his lap? I turned to Jerry and said, "Oh, my God, Jerry, why didn't you tell me? I have been standing right here next to him all this time and didn't know it!" Poor

Jerry! He didn't know <u>what</u> to say. My knees weakened and I
thought I was going to faint. Talk about hurt! I was stunned!
A second later the pair got up and started to leave, and as
they went out the door, I mustered my courage and went after
them. I caught up with them in the courtyard of the apartment
building and cried out to him, "What are you <u>doing</u>?… Why are
<u>you</u> doing <u>this</u>?" He turned around and stared blankly at me,
as though he didn't know who I was. (BUT HE KNEW… OF
COURSE, HE DID!) I realized he was kind of drunk, and the
girl kept pulling on him saying, "Come on, Sweetie, let's get
out of here. Forget about her. Come on, Baby, let's go! Come
on!" Then I sort of lost it and went right up in his face and said,
"You give me <u>forty</u> dollars, **right now**!" "Why do <u>you</u> want
forty dollars?" I said, "It cost me twenty dollars to get out here,
and it will cost me twenty to get back! Now <u>give</u> it to me!"
Reluctantly he did, while this dizzy dame kept pulling on him,
calling him "Baby" and "Sweetie." Then they left together, and
I just stood there gasping and stunned, as I watched them drive
away.

I went back into the apartment and found Jerry. He wanted to help me as he could see I was in a state of shock and disbelief. It didn't make any sense… Why had Nitschke called me at my hotel in the first place? My fellow must have asked him to call me. But why? Just to get me there, and then hurt me? I now understood why Nitschke had seemingly discouraged me from going into the party. He knew what was going on inside and how upset I would be. What a dirty, rotten thing to do to a sweet, little, ole,' country girl from Wisconsin. RIGHT? And, to a loyal Packer fan. Perhaps the fellow was teaching me… if I wanted to play with the "big boys," I had better learn how to take the punishment. But I surely wasn't ready for this. (*AH, come on, fella, have a heart*!) A heart… Ahhhh!… now there's the problem… a heart… an affair of the heart. So that's why I hurt so much… I was in love and my heart was breaking. Big mistake, Sandy!

Jerry fixed a stiff drink for me and by then the party was closing down and people were leaving. I asked Jerry to get me out of there, and he thought he was doing the correct thing by not letting me go back to my hotel alone. I was not functioning well and was far too upset to be left by myself. We got a cab and gave Paul's ex-wife a ride home. I would not let myself cry in front of her, but the moment she got out of the cab…oh! Man! Boo Hoo! So, my good ole' friend, Jerry… not knowing what to do with me, took me back to his hotel where the team was staying. Bigger mistake! Right, Jerry? By this time I was feeling the drinks and crying inconsolably. Jerry took me to his room and woke up his roommate and my friend, Willie Davis. Willie asked us what had happened and when I started to tell him, I cried even harder. Willie tried to calm me down and make me be quiet. Both of them were afraid I would wake Vince Lombardi, and if I did, Lombardi would blow his stack. Finally, Jerry or Willie, I don't know which, called up my fellow, the one who had hurt me, and told him this was his problem… not theirs. They said I was in their room, crying uncontrollably, and I was going to wake up Vince, and they told him to come and get me… right away. I was somewhat gratified the dizzy dame was no longer with him, and I wondered what had become of her, but he immediately came to get me, although he had trouble getting me quietly down the hall to his room. I was beyond pain and hurt, and I felt like I was dying! Here was this wonderful person whom I loved… how could he have done such a <u>despicable</u> thing to me? Didn't he know me well enough to realize I wasn't tough enough for this? Didn't he know how much he could hurt me? I believed in him and really cared for him, and he was sooo cute! WHY? I fell asleep in his bed with his arms around me. A few minutes later the phone rang. "HELLO!" and he and his roommate got up and left. It was time for the team to get on the plane and go back to Green Bay. There I was, alone in a strange hotel room in Dallas, TX and I had no idea where the hotel was located. I was not looking or feeling very well and when I got outside… it was so <u>blasted</u> **hot**. I got a cab, and sure enough, it cost me $20 to get back to my hotel. Believe it or not, the sweet nephew of Lee Roy Caffey, the one I had sat next to at the game, called me at my hotel and he could tell I was upset, so he came to see me. The poor kid! I cried to him, also! He helped me pack my bags while I told him what had happened, and his eyes became the size of saucers! I probably destroyed all of his healthy and beautiful visions of the great and wonderful football heroes his Uncle Lee Roy had told him about. (*If you're reading this now, kid, <u>sorry</u>, but thanks for helping me and giving me a shoulder to cry on.*) He put me in a cab and sent me on my way to Love's

Field. It seemed as though I had to walk a million miles to get to my plane…and it was so <u>damned</u> **hot!** The first thing I asked the flight attendant for was an air sickness bag… and believe me, I used it!

Maybe this has happened to you, maybe not … I certainly hope <u>not</u>. If it has, well, it is a real killer, isn't it? When I think about it now, I realize I should have known better from the beginning and it serves me right. This guy was a cocky, young rooster who had a bunch of hens in his barnyard! He had a girl in every town the Packers played. He used <u>me</u> to boost his ego, that's all! …and I had certainly spent a lot of time doing that…boosting his ego. I am the one who <u>continually</u> told him how great he was. Me… ME…**ME!** I don't think he realized how much he really cared about me or needed me, until I was gone. I know <u>now</u> it wouldn't have worked out for us. Sure, I was in <u>love</u> with him, but he was <u>not</u> in <u>love</u> with me. (*Gee, no kidding? What was your first clue?*) Well, too bad, sailor! You missed out on a special gal! Funny thing though, it has been over thirty-five years, and I still have never quite gotten over the hurt I felt that night in Dallas. It made me cautious, and I still have feelings of humiliation and down-right <u>disbelief</u> that someone I loved could be so hurtful to me. But damn… he was sooo cute! Obviously, I didn't marry this football hero, although at one time I certainly wanted to. Curses, foiled again! (*Yes …yes, okay, I hear you, Lord. I'll say it!*) …"Thank you."

BUT HE'S <u>SOOO</u> CUTE!

Have you noticed how many of the football players get <u>special</u> attention because I think they're "CUTE?" In fact I have mentioned their <u>cuteness</u> several times, but as I get older I question my rationale. What is wrong with me? It seems if a guy is **<u>cute</u>** … it must mean he is absolutely wonderful. Why can men get away with so much just because we think they're **<u>cute</u>**? My friend and lawyer, Jack McManus, of Fairbanks, AK and Madison, WI has discussed this with me many times. He tells of women coming to him for legal assistance because of abuse. The women complain to him, and tell him their husbands or boyfriends beat them and abuse them. When he asks them why they stay with him, they say, "Because he's sooo **<u>CUTE</u>**." Come on, ladies, enough already!!! It is this kind of thinking that is getting some of us hurt.

Here is my suggestion! The next time a fellow shows up who is **<u>CUTE,</u>** stop and think before you fall for him. Wouldn't it make a lot more sense, and be less difficult, to find a PLAIN LOOKING man who is kind, sweet, generous, faithful, loving, and smart, with the potential of making lots of big bucks? …Maybe even a nerd? If you can't stand the way he looks put a paper bag over his head while you're making love to him. <u>Guys</u> talk about "brown-bagging" women all the time. So, ladies, why can't we?

Then you marry the guy! You <u>love him</u> good and <u>spoil him</u> rotten so he cannot possibly survive without you, and you help him make his fortune. Then when you're rich enough, take him to a plastic surgeon and have him fixed the way you want him to look. Which is… of course… **"<u>CUTE</u>"**! Also, you are now wealthy enough to afford any nips and tucks you might want or need for yourself. So just do it! Get it done and make yourself **<u>cute</u>**, too! You deserve it, you beautiful doll! Okay, now! So, let's consider it!

In my opinion Ray Nitschke was not sooo cute... to me, he was "beautiful." I miss his hugs!
Collection of Vernon Biever (copyright)

271

THE TRANSITION

Finally, I had accomplished something worthwhile in my life... I graduated from college! I finished in three years, instead of the usual four or five which it normally takes. I took large credit loads so I could finish sooner, because in truth, I was worried I wouldn't make it. When I finished I realized how foolish I was to have hurried, as I enjoyed the college experience and would have made it without all the unnecessary pressure I had placed on myself. Once I received the "sheepskin" I still did not know what I wanted to do, so I decided to go to Graduate School at the University of Wisconsin in Madison, and major in Public Address and Communications.

One time during this period, I heard Paul Hornung announce a football game on the radio. He was not playing football anymore, but had pursued a career in radio and television as a sports announcer/commentator. When the speaker said, "This is Paul Hornung," I couldn't believe my ears. It didn't sound like him until I listened for awhile, and then, I could detect the slight Louisville, KY accent which Paul still carried. The register of his voice was much <u>lower</u>, and either he had come-of-age all over again, or he had taken some speech and voice lessons to lower the register and help his communication skills... he sounded good! I was pleased for him, so I wrote him a little note in care of the Packer office, and told him how impressed I was with what I had heard. I was graduating from college with a degree in Speech and Drama so I knew a little bit about public speaking, and I felt I was qualified to comment on his performance. About two weeks after I wrote the letter, I came home one day and my roommate said I had received a phone call. She said, "A man called to tell you 'Thanks for the letter!'" "Well, who was it?" I asked. "All he said is, 'Tell Sandy that Paul called... her old friend from Green Bay.'" That was all... I knew his marriage was over, and I realized Paul was going through a transition, too.

My transition took place in August 1969, when I moved to Madison and <u>hurriedly</u> found an apartment. The first year of Grad School was the year from "hell" (1969-1970) and my roommate, also acquired in a <u>hurry</u>, was difficult for me to live with. There was a Teaching Assistant's walk-out (strike) at the University during the fall semester, and as a result of having no teachers, we seldom held class, though students showed up at the classrooms, stayed 15 minutes, and then left. I didn't learn much during the entire year, other than the fact I do not like any form of domestic or civil unrest. I like peace, but most people do and then, in the spring semester the "crap" really did <u>hit the fan</u>. Peace protests and peace signs were everywhere, but it was not <u>peaceful</u>, as major riots and demonstrations interrupted campus life, and, on the Kent State College campus in Ohio, the National Guard carried loaded weapons (May-1970). When the National Guard had been provoked to the breaking point, a young Guardsman who was probably frightened and overly-anxious, opened fire on a crowd of students, killing two of them. The country went wild with anger, disgust, confusion, and criticism over the incident and I was afraid a similar thing would happen at UW-Madison, as the stage was set for the same type of tragedy. On one side were the enraged students protesting the war, and on the other were the soldiers (most of them the same age as the students), harboring diverse allegiances, standing in opposition, and both were defending their beliefs in liberty. Americans all! The insults and taunting from unarmed student protestors was enough to drive the soldiers to a breaking point, and the soldiers, though the guns were not loaded in Wisconsin, were nevertheless, carrying guns. It was tense, and I felt sure something was going to happen, and it wasn't going to be good. While using the demonstrations and riots in Madison and at the University of California-Berkley as a source of reference, most of the more-adult population looked down their noses at the college students, and loudly labeled all of us "radicals." Not all of us were radical, and many of us were deeply concerned over the war and voiced our opinions in a quiet, orderly manner. There were non-violent protests, which I sometimes attended, but the Kent State incident was vivid in my mind, and I was often afraid to let my beliefs be known. It is sad when U.S. citizens, having the right to peacefully assemble and speak freely, do so, and are then gunned down on a college campus. I'll bet our forefathers were rolling in their graves. Our country was in the midst of troubled times, and the conflict over the justice of the Viet Nam War effected all U.S. citizens. I know of no one who was not touched in some way by the war and unrest.

As an example of the chaos, one afternoon I was kicked and shoved as I left the Van Hise classroom building. Someone yelled that ABC News cameras were filming on the other side of the UW-Bascom Hall, and after hearing that announcement, a group of students behind me tried to push through the doors so they could get to the rally over the hill, become involved, and seen on camera, and, it was frightening for me to witness the mob mentality. Later that year, a protest bomb exploded in the University's Chemistry Building right across the street from Van Hise, and a student researcher was killed. The bomber, Carlton Armstrong, escaped to Canada after a nationwide manhunt.

That spring, during my performance in a play at the UW

Student Union, the National Guard contended with a riot outside the building. They were using tear gas and mace to control the crowd, and the fumes came in through the cracks in the windows and doors, and I choked on stage, as did other actors and some of the audience. It was scary to walk around the campus and I remember having to stay inside a restaurant with a wet towel over my face because they were gassing the students who were rioting outside.

The leaders of The Students for a Democratic Society were traveling between the campuses at Madison and Berkeley, CA, and every day, assembled a protest on the Campus Mall, and handed out pamphlets and gave speeches condemning the U.S. Government's participation in Nam. Everyone was on edge… I hated the War, and I hated the war zone which was now the University of Wisconsin Campus. I had known fellow-students who had gone to fight, and some came home battered, with horror stories… while a few acquaintances did not come back at all. I did not know what to do about the situation other than to get on with my life the best way I could, and at the time that meant continuing with my education. However, education is a difficult undertaking when there are military trucks with soldiers aboard everywhere on the Campus. I remember parking about 2 miles away and walking in, because one could not drive a vehicle on the Campus grounds and military helicopters patrolled overheard. Needless to say, it was not a very "FUN" year… interesting and exciting, but definitely, not <u>fun</u>.

I now lived further away from Green Bay, so I did not go there very often. I did not have the time to go because Graduate School at Madison is tough, as it should be. It seemed as though most of the Packer players I had known were retiring from football, and many were attempting other careers. Boyd Dowler played football one more year at Green Bay, and then became a player/coach with the L.A. Rams. Ray Nitschke was one of the only ones left whom I had known from the Lombardi years… even Lombardi was gone. One by one they had said "good-bye." I did not like college in Madison… I was lonely and unhappy and it was a bad time in my life, and the lives of many others.

One day after class in the spring of 1970, I received a phone call from my cousin, Gordon. He was calling from a little bar in Montello, WI and he said, "Hi, Sweetheart, you will <u>never</u> guess who I am sitting next to." I was feeling "down in the dumps" and I didn't want to guess. "Here, I'll let you say 'hello' to him yourself." A moment later I heard a man with a deep voice say, "Hello, Sandra, this is Danny." No Way! How could it be? It was Dan Currie, but what was he doing in Montello, WI? I had seen him only one time since he had been traded to the Los Angeles Rams in 1964. "What are you doing here, Danny?" "A friend and I came to Wisconsin on business. His father owns some lettuce and mint farms here, and we're going to stay for awhile." At some point in the conversation I picked up on the fact he was divorced, and I said, "Stay where you are. I'll be there in 2 hours." That was another "defining moment" in my life and two hours later, when I arrived, almost everything in my life changed.

. . . .

It did not take me long to figure out Dan was having a difficult time in his life. He had been working in Miami at a stock brokerage company called Woodstock, Inc., and apparently, a group of con-men had set up a "sting" on Dan's employer by running a bogus check through Woodstock's bank account; the check was made out for $2.5 million. There were a number of Chicago gangsters, believed to be associated with the Mafia, who were part of the swindle. Eventually it was alleged that on or around December 10, 1969, a bank clearing house in Chicago had accepted the check payable to one, "Jack Walsh" (a non-existing person), and the check was supposedly endorsed by Dan's boss. (It was a counterfeit signature.) The funds from the forged check were placed in an escrow account, and the Chicago clearing house had begun to make disbursements from the account. "Inside" men (the bad guys) cleared the payments through the system until the theft was eventually noticed. Close to $1,000,000,000 had vanished before the "run" was detected and halted.

Dan had no idea what was happening, and he came to work one morning to find the FBI waiting for him and the other employees; the door of his office was locked and barred. Naturally, Dan was a suspect, and Bill Quinlan, who was working with Dan at the same company was, also, an FBI suspect. They were harassed, investigated, and of course, scared. As a result, Bill went home to Lawrence, MA and Dan decided to come to Wisconsin with his employer, where they were going to file a law suit against the clearing house in Chicago. They wanted to sue <u>somebody</u>… <u>anybody</u>… they were totally frustrated. I have no recollection how far the lawsuit went, or if one was actually filed, but I do remember it was a complicated mess! For Dan…it was a bad dream … come true.

In short, Dan Currie was broke, had gone through a divorce, missed his children terribly, and was generally, just-plain… "down on his luck." Bad things <u>can</u> happen and often do, and I am reminded of a book by author, Harold S. Kushner, "When Bad Things Happen To Good People." (1980) Dan is, in my opinion, "good people," so I did everything I could to help him during these rough times.

To say he was "battered and bruised" is an understatement. He also suffered psychologically; he had trouble sleeping, and when he did sleep, he had "horrific" nightmares. He continually dreamed he was on a beach with his children in his arms, and big dogs were attacking them. He jumped at the least little thing which startled him. He was afraid to turn out the lights at night, so he dozed on the couch with the lights on.

My heart went out to him; I was going to save him, and I was very soon committed to him, and "CRAZY" about him. Maybe I had always been a little crazy about him, but in the past I would not allow myself to feel anything for him because he was married. And now, here **I** was… lonely, not getting any younger, and needing someone to love and care for. All of my female instincts were aroused. And NOW, here **he** was… and I finally had a chance with someone… a football hero. Of course, the situation was not idyllic, but I refused to acknowledge the difference between this and an ideal relationship. After all, what *is* an ideal relationship? Who can tell me? It's different for each person, but analyzing it now, our relationship was doomed. I felt as though I was blindly running around on the ground, looking up, trying to catch someone who was falling.

Sure, Dan was <u>single</u>… he was "free!" "**Free**" with a big price tag on him. Dan was definitely not a "good catch" considering all the <u>baggage</u> the poor guy was carrying around… but still, I cared for him, and I was hoping beyond hope, he would get a <u>good</u> break somewhere along the line, and if that happened we would be all right, and everything could be justified.

He was honest with me and discouraged our relationship; telling me I would be wasting my time with him. He tried to make me realize he had nothing to offer me, but, being an eternal optimist, I would not allow myself to see the truth about the situation. I don't easily take "NO" for an answer, I love a challenge, and no one could convince me this relationship was <u>not</u> "okay." It didn't make any difference to me how bad things were for him… I was convinced I could make it better. I wanted him… and <u>that</u> was <u>that</u>.

pointer

students, faculty, administra.

)NSIN STATE UNIVERSITY, STEVENS POINT, WISCONSIN, OCTOBER 13, 1966

neman was active in "Showboat," "Music Man" and many other productions. Miss Finney played lead roles in "Medea," Mary Stuart and "Arsenic and Old Lace" in Beaver.

Jane Liljestrand, a transfer from University of Wisconsin-Marinette Center, was active with the UW touring o p e r a group and with the UW Children's Theater. Diane Benzschawel just back from a summer in Europe, brings theater experience to us from Whitewater State University.

The 18 College Theater men in Bernarda Alba's House are all backstage because it is an all-girl show. Reading this large production staff as stage manager is another transfer student, Earl Smith, who comes here via the Air Force and Hardin-Simmons University in Texas. A fine actor and dancer Mr. S m i t h was featured this past summer as Henry VII in "A Man For All Seasons," the l e a d in "The Guardsman," and served as choreographer for "Ondine" for the WSU Summer Theater.

Mr. Smith's staff heads include Steve Rees — master carpenter; Doug Wisby — master electrician; Diane Benzschawel — property mistress; Sandra Fischer — costumes; John Davis — sound technician; and College Theater president, John Primm — makeup chairman. Students present ID card at box office for a free ticket.

SANDY YOUNG, our own Green Bay Packer, will appear in "The House of Bernarda Alba."

I made the front page of the college newspaper. WOW!

My beautiful mother and me on my college graduation day. June - 1969.

A FRONT ROW SEAT

"It was the best of times…it was the worst of times," begins
Charles Dickens' book, The Tale of Two Cities. (1859) Had
Dickens been writing about us, Dan Currie and Sandy Young,
he would probably have begun with the same sentence. It
was the best of times, especially for me… it was the worst of
times… for Dan… but his problems did not stop us from having
a good time.

I was pleased to have such a handsome, exciting football
hero in my life. We lived in Madison, WI and once it became
known Dan was back, the calls and invitations started to roll
in. Though he had been absent from football for about 5 years,
the Packer organization, his teammates, friends, and fans had

certainly not forgotten him. Many of the Madison in-crowd
quickly adopted him as one of their own, and it amazed me
how little time it took for Dan to become part of the Madison
social scene… his celebrity played an important role in this.
He frequented Madison's favorite watering holes and spent a
good deal of time at the University of Wisconsin Field House,
talking with coaches and Wisconsin Alumni; gravitating to
high-profile people and they to him. I was seldom missing from
Dan's arm, and though I sometimes had a little trouble keeping
up with him, I relished the limelight. He called me "Princess"
and usually made me feel like one. On occasion he called me
"Flora Dora" because I liked to dress up, and never went out of
the house without make up on my face, and my hair coifed. He
quickly notified all male acquaintances that I was meant to be
his "belle of the ball."

Though I was with him much of the time, Dan is a man's
man, and he still enjoyed the BS and drinking with the boys
while I, like all possessive females, wanted him to be at home
with me… as often as possible. Naturally, there was always
a struggle as to who would win out in this battle… me or the

boys. Once, in order to get him home, I used some female psychology on him. He didn't own a car at the time and he depended on the boys to drive him home, which was also just another excuse and a way for the boys to have control over him, keeping him out with them. So early one evening, I called a popular place where I knew he was drinking and asked to speak with him. When he got on the phone, I whispered to him in the sexiest voice I could muster and said, "Hi! Sweetheart! You know, I really feel like making love…" "Yeah, so!" he said. I softly replied, "…and I <u>prefer</u>… that it be with <u>you</u>." There was a moment of silence while he digested what I had said, and then he hollered, "Stay right where you are… don't move… I'll be right home!" I found out later he had run up and down the bar trying to borrow a car from someone. Somehow he managed to get home within the hour and it tickled me, and though it was meant to be a little trick, it was gratifying to know his response …it told me he cared. We had fun telling this story to other people when they curiously inquired about our relationship.

Another thing bothering Dan was not being in Green Bay during the years of the first Super Bowls and with the

teammates he <u>loved</u> so much. Though it was hidden, the hurt
(inflicted when Lombardi traded him to the Los Angeles
Rams in 1964), involved the <u>loss</u> of his <u>football</u> family, <u>loss</u> of
recognition, and the <u>loss</u> of his involvement in the "glory days"
which his efforts had helped create, and it was a wound which
still festered just under the surface. We drank too much, and
often after a night of boozing, the old sore would be re-opened,
and I was never sure what to expect when Dan's frustration
reached a boiling point. Sometimes I was concerned about the
possible consequences, and at times it seemed as though he
blamed me for what had happened to him. Perhaps I would be
more correct to say that because he wanted a better life for us
as a couple… my presence, only reminded him that things were
<u>not</u> so great. Of course I didn't help the situation because often,
I drank too much also, and I hadn't the brains to keep my big
mouth shut when I should have. I am sure that I unwittingly
added to his frustrations.

When we were <u>not</u> drinking we had wonderful times
together. We often went on picnics, boated with friends, went
ice-skating (he was an experienced ice skater and a hockey

player) and Dan spent hours preparing special, gourmet meals for me…he loved to try new recipes. We memorized poetry, sang and danced, and worked out a song and dance routine for the song, "Everything's Coming Up Roses," which together, we were frequently asked to perform at the end of a night of partying. We loved the theatre and show business in general, and we spent time and money taking in every production we could afford in the Madison and Milwaukee area, often taking in local <u>high</u> <u>school</u> productions. When we went to a musical we would mimic the songs and routines at home for a few weeks, until another production caught our interest.

We bought a Shih Tzu puppy and named her "Duffy," after Duffy Dougherty, Dan's college football coach. The dog could fit into Dan's hand and several Madison residents, who had to pass by our place early in the morning, commented and chuckled about seeing Dan walk the dog; a great, big, tall man, seemingly being <u>led</u> down the street by this teeny, tiny, little puppy dog.

In ways, it was a wonderful partnership and we worked at

making our home comfortable. I was fortunate because Dan liked to vacuum and did much of the housekeeping for me. He was great at taking out the trash and handling the heavier work, and that's how he got some of his exercise. He was immaculate in his personal habits, and I learned that when he was younger, he had cared for his invalid mother, and because of this, he was domesticated and was not in any way threatened by doing what is referred to by some as, "woman's work"… Dan was all man. One heavy job was however, all mine, and it was picking up Dan's shoes which he often left around the apartment or by the front door. He wears a size 14E and the shoes were so heavy, I tired from gathering all of them, and putting them away.

He helped me with my college master's degree classes in Education, and I spent time tutoring him for the various insurance exams which were required to license him as an insurance agent. Pat O'Donahue, a former football star at the University of Wisconsin, San Francisco 49er's, and Packers, had an agency in Madison, and he gave Dan a job and tried to get him established in the insurance business.

As a couple, it was obvious we <u>loved</u> each other, and many people thought we would marry… we went to Church and prayed together, as sincere couples often do. My parents were fond of Dan and vice-versa and we spent a great deal of time with my mother and father, meeting them for dinner at different restaurants around the State, or for picnics in various beautiful Wisconsin settings. I love the story about my father which Dan has told so many times. The first time I brought Dan home to meet my parents, my father asked him what he would like for a cocktail and Dan asked for a Dry Martini, straight-up. My father gave him a very small, <u>wet</u> Martini in a tiny, little glass, and then he proceeded to fix for himself, a 15 oz. Perfect Brandy Manhattan, heavy on the sweet, in a huge gobbler. Dan swallowed the Martini in one gulp, and patiently waited for my father to finish his drink, and then expected both glasses… to be refilled. When my father finished his drink, he rose from his easy chair, and Dan handed him his glass. My father said, "The drinking light is out! Time for dinner!" Dan said he learned his lesson <u>quickly</u> and the next time he came to our house and my father asked, "What will you have to drink, Dan?" Dan quickly responded, "Whatever <u>you're</u> having, Harold!"

Mother was sure that any day, Dan and I would simply go to a judge, and get married. But we never got around to it… maybe because we both knew that deep down, and for many reasons, it wasn't the right thing to do.

In 1971, soon after we got together in Madison, I began encouraging Dan to tell his story. He contacted an old schoolmate, Jack Winter, who was a professional writer with many contacts in the entertainment world. With Dan's and my input, Jack put together Dan's story and eventually, Ed Sabol, and his son, Steve, of NFL Films, Inc., journeyed to Wisconsin and filmed a short history of Dan's football career.

One of the most memorable weekends of my life occurred when NFL Films came to Wisconsin to shoot Dan's story (1972). On Wednesday or Thursday, Jack Winter, who once wrote for the TV show, American Sportsman, came to town to set up the logistics for the shoot. On Friday, the crew of NFL Films arrived, and on Saturday, we went to Milton College where some filming was done on the sidelines as Dan helped

coach the Saturday afternoon game along with his friend
and Michigan State teammate, Rudy Gaddini, Milton's head
football coach.

In the evenings we partied. Oh, boy, did we party! All of
us; most of the film crew, Jack, and Dan and I went to Fuzzy
Thurston's Left Guard in Madison on Friday and Saturday
nights. The Left Guard always had a great band and the drinks
flowed often and generously. On one of these nights Jack
Winter met a little, 19 year old "cutie" on the dance floor, and
they fell instantly in love, and from then on, wherever we went,
she went also.

We were going to shoot a film segment in Milwaukee at
the Packer game in County Stadium during the Monday Night
Football broadcast. Late Sunday afternoon many of the people
involved met at Fuzzy's Left Guard in Milwaukee for dinner.
Paul Hornung, Max McGee, Ed and Steve Sabol, and Dan and I
were seated at a round table for eight, as were Jack Winter and
the "little number" he had recently picked up in Madison. I was
seated on one side of Jack Winter and the girl was on his other

side, and Paul Hornung sat next to her.

I recall ordering the least expensive dish ($5.) on the menu because I did not know who would be picking up the check, and I wanted to be kind and go easy on the person who would get the honors. As we were ordering the girl became emotional, saying she was a vegetarian and could not eat any of the predominately "meaty" selections on the menu. To rescue her and calm her down, all the men pitched in and suggested that she have a lobster, which was Market Priced at about $25. I would have liked a lobster, too, but I had not asked for one. *You big dumbie!* Once she was appeased, we enjoyed our drinks and dinner, as well as the delightful banter which goes on when a group such as this get together. The girl had been talking to Paul throughout the meal and when it came time for dessert, she leaned over to Jack Winter (her date) and whispered something in his ear. Jack's face flushed and he turned to me and said, almost in her defense, "She wants to go to bed with Hornung. What should I say? I suppose I should say, 'Go Ahead!' The poor kid may never have a chance like this again." I was "ticked," probably because I was now 31 years old and no

longer 19 or, maybe because of the lobster or, maybe because
I had competition at a table of all men or, maybe because she
was being rotten and inconsiderate to her date, my new-found
friend, Jack Winter. I am not sure which of these statements
would be most accurate, and perhaps all of them ring true, but
nevertheless, I was still "ticked," a little envious, and very
disgusted. Paul knew what was going on, but I don't think he
instigated an invitation to sleep with him. Of course he didn't
discourage it either. I just shrugged my shoulders and said in
a loud voice, certainly at least loud enough for Paul to hear,
"What do you want me to say, Jack? I was 19 once, too!"

On Monday evening after the Monday Night Football
telecast many of us went to dinner at Frenchy's Restaurant, a
very popular and elegant Milwaukee eatery and gathering place.
Dan and I were seated at a long table with the Sabols, Jack
Winter, and others, and next to us, at an equally long table, sat
Howard Cosell, Frank Gifford, "Dandy" Don Meredith, ABC's
celebrated young producer, Don Olmeyer, and other members
of the staff of Monday Night Football. We bantered back and
forth and had a ball. After dinner I pulled my chair out from

the table and turned it so I could join in with the Monday Night Football fellows, and Howard Cosell pulled his chair out to meet me. Howard and I engaged in a somewhat intellectual discussion but I cannot remember what it concerned. All I remember is Howard and I could converse really well and it was thrilling for me. At the end of the night, after enjoying a sumptuous repast, we all started to leave but Frenchy's owners stalled us and held a drawing for a door prize. Frank Gifford won, and the prize, a huge stuffed teddy bear, was larger than him. It was gigantic! Everyone roared with laughter, teasing Frank about his new date, the big bear, and joking that Frank would not be going to his room all alone on this particular night. (Frank was single at the time!) Someone summoned a taxi for Frank and we stuffed him in, along with the bear. Once inside we could no longer see Frank, and as the cab pulled away all one could see was this huge bear's head (facing front) in the back window of the cab. It looked as though the bear was all by himself. We stood there, watching the departure into the night, as we held our sides… laughing.

I know who got Frank, many years later… Kathie Lee, but

I've often wondered who ended up with the bear. Incidentally, Paul and the girl never showed for the Monday night dinner. I wonder where they ended up or if they ever got together! Your guess is as good as mine!

We hoped for feedback from the NFL program which might result in a coaching position, but there was no feedback from the story. However, we certainly had fun putting it together. Ed Sabol wrote to us later telling how much he, too, had enjoyed the filming of the "Dan Currie Epic," as he referred to it in his letter, because of the many parties and a lot of laughing behind the scenes in which Ed, and son, Steve, took part. The Sabols were absolutely wonderful to Dan and me, and I am thrilled by their continued success, and for the <u>history of professional football</u> which they have ingeniously recorded, and preserved for the ages in NFL FILM libraries.

In those years Fuzzy Thurston sponsored a foundation called the Thousand Yard Club, which honored athletes who had gained 1,000 yards in the NFL. It began as a golf tournament and modest dinner function, but it wasn't too many years before it became so popular, successful, and large in attendance, the banquet had to be held in the Outagamie County Airport <u>Hanger</u> in Appleton to accommodate the crowd. Dan and I were invited, but the women (wives and girlfriends were not allowed at the banquet) went out to dinner together, and waited for the fellows to return to the Appleton Left Guard when it was over.

I recall, after one of the banquets I was sitting in a back room of the Left Guard at a table with Susan Ann Thurston, Fuzzy's wife, Sue Meredith, Don Meridith's wife, and Marguerite Simpson, O.J. Simpson's wife, and others. We were laughing and having a great time, talking, drinking, and watching Don Meredith clown around on stage after he had returned from the banquet. Don had strapped on a guitar and was pantomiming Elvis Presley, and he was good, too! Suddenly the door opened and in walked O.J. Simpson. He was unbelievable.... tall and good-looking, he stood in the doorway...making a Grand Entrance. I think he knew the first impression we women would have of him, so he stood there and milked it for all it was worth... at least, it seemed like it to me. Each of the women sitting at the table met one another's

eyes, giving each other an all-knowing look which said…
"Ooh, my gawd, what a beautiful man!" O.J. was attired in all-white… shirt and slacks… and… the shirt had big, full, bolero sleeves and the pants were form-fitting. The shirt was left open to the waist and displayed his gorgeous, golden-colored chest. Around his neck were layers and layers of different-length gold chains. You could see all of the women at the table gawk at him, and when their blood pressure rose, some blushed and became subdued, dropping their eyes to focus on their drinks. We all knew what the other was thinking, but after all, we were sitting at the table with O.J.'s adoring wife, Marguerite, but I knew some envied her. I will never forget years later when I was watching the now famous, white, Ford Bronco chase of O.J. Simpson and the L.A. police, right after Nicole Brown's murder, and a television news reporter got Marguerite on the phone. I think he expected her to be critical of O.J and to be calm and logical… after all, she was the spurned <u>ex</u>-wife. I was startled and stunned when she hysterically screamed into the phone, "Run, O.J., RUN!" just as though he was on the field running with a football. I don't know what I expected her to say but, I could certainly tell her feelings for him had never waned.

The news reporter cut her off immediately… and I could tell by his fumbling dialogue, he too, was surprised by her reaction.

I called and spoke to my friend, Jackie Nitschke, Ray Nitschke's wife, about the Simpson trial while it was going on, and I asked her what <u>was</u> the word around the League regarding O.J.'s guilt or innocence. Jackie said, "We all know he did it!" She then reminded me I had seen this type of rage in Dan, and that she also, had seen it in Ray. She was right… I had… and though I felt terrible about the murders, I understood that one of these huge, muscular fellows, if provoked to the limit, was physically capable of doing great harm to another human being. If circumstances warranted, many were capable of extreme violence, but most all others had harnessed their strength… and rage… and contained it; only to expend it on a football field, never allowing it to surge uncontrolled, off the field. Jackie Nitschke had taken a young barbarian (Ray) who was full of rage and violence, had channeled his explosive energy, and had patiently molded him into a big, soft piece of milk toast, <u>off the field</u>.

Being Dan Currie's girlfriend put me in a <u>front row seat</u> (right where I had always wanted to be) at many exciting events. One such event was Bart Starr Day which was designated to honor our famous and revered Lombardi quarterback. Richard M. Nixon, President of the United States, came to Green Bay to pay tribute; an emergency plan, in case of catastrophe, was put into operation in Green Bay, while everyone had to have security clearance in order to get into the function at which Nixon would honor Bart Starr.

Specially invited dignitaries and the Packer Alumni attended a cocktail party held right before we were to board buses, which would take us to the Brown County Auditorium where Nixon would speak. At the party, I mingled around talking with everyone, and Dan began prodding me, hurrying me along so we could get on the bus, and perhaps have a chance for a better seat at the Nixon event. As it turned out, my delay caused us to be some of the last people to board the bus. Dan scolded me and said when in circumstances like this, I must stay alert, be aware, move quickly, and not be left behind. (*Yes, Sir!*) Because we were the last on the bus, we were the first off, and as we filed out, we were escorted into the auditorium, entering from behind the stage, and ushers began filling the front row seats <u>first</u> with the some of the <u>first</u> people to enter the building… and Dan and myself. As the seats filled from the far-end of the first row, he and I found our seats… directly in front of the podium where Nixon would appear and speak.

I was nervous after being scolded, and also, because I had visions of someone attacking the President. (Remember, it had been <u>less</u> than 10 years since John Kennedy had been assassinated.) I anxiously began swinging my crossed-leg in anticipation of his entrance. I was wearing a fashionable pair of new, white, knee-high boots and a mini-skirt. When Nixon entered and began to speak, I sat down and again started subconsciously swinging my booted legs… first one and then the other. He could not help but look down and notice me while he spoke… I was smiling, swinging the leg, and I suppose I was trying to evoke confidence, and show him we were a friendly crowd. So I smiled at him continually, and he kept smiling back at me. When the ceremony concluded he descended the stage and quickly shook hands with those in the front row, and <u>seemed</u> to be hurrying to the middle to get to me. He

shook Dan's hand first, and then he grabbed my hand, leaned

slightly into me and softly said, "Hello there… so you must

be the <u>CHERRY</u> of the evening." Dan and I were surprised…

and taken aback… and then Dan started to say something,

almost in rebuttal… but the secret service man caught what

was happening, and moved the President along. We have never

been quite sure what Nixon meant, although, I know the remark

was not meant to be mean-spirited. Later, some of the Packer

couples and Dan and I guessed, that since Bart Starr's wife's

name is Cherry, most likely Nixon was acknowledging me as

Dan's… wife, or his significant other. We will never know for

sure, but nevertheless, I had been in a <u>front row seat</u>.

Another event which was thrilling was the very first Vince

Lombardi Memorial Golf Classic, which was held at the North

Hills Country Club in Menomonee Falls, just northwest of

Milwaukee. Dan was pleased and proud to be invited and

was equally delighted he had this wonderful event to which

he could take me. He knew I would relish every moment;

the preparation, as well as the actual event. The charity golf committee had invited some of the Lombardi players, and also many, famous, Hollywood celebrities to golf with the sponsors of the tournament.

I bought a new gown to wear to the banquet, went on a diet, and made sure I had a gorgeous tan. We shopped for a baby-blue tuxedo for Dan, matching my dress, and he too took time to make sure he was groomed and was physically Top-Notch.

We were given a brand new Buick to drive as a courtesy car, and a beautiful room in the Pfister Hotel, downtown Milwaukee, as were the other celebrities. In those years we were spending a lot of time with Ray and Jackie Nitschke, and Dan had recently called Ray and asked him to be his Best Man when he married me… and Ray had obliged. The tee off time for Ray was scheduled for early in the morning which gave Ray plenty of time to finish his 18 holes of golf at North Hills, have lunch, leisurely go back downtown to the hotel, dress for the banquet, and bring Jackie and himself back to the Country Club for the Cocktail Hour and Banquet. Since it was the very first Tournament, the planners of the event had not considered the plight of those who teed off last, considering how they were supposed to make it downtown to shower, dress, and rush back for the party. Dan was in the <u>last</u> foursome to tee off, and because of this he knew he would be very rushed and late for the Cocktail Hour and the evening's festivities. He was upset over this… and he called me at the hotel to explain … and he caught up with Ray on the golf course, instructing him to bring his dress clothes and me, along with Jackie and himself, and meet him in the Country Club Locker Room as early as possible.

Everything went as planned and I rode out in my gorgeous gown with Ray and Jackie, who were equally well attired. We giggled about Dan being disgruntled, but when we arrived I noticed Ray sensed trouble, and he went immediately to the Locker Room to give Dan his evening clothes. A little while later when Dan entered the room, he looked magnificent. I greeted him, but I could tell he was boiling <u>inside</u>, and he went right over to the bar and ordered a Martini. Oh, No! I groaned, knowing the results if he stayed with the Martinis all evening… but there was no stopping him. I too had my share of drinks but

was aware of the crowd, and didn't want to over-indulge and
make a fool of myself.

At the end of the evening… (a delightful experience, with all
the Hollywood celebrities partaking)… we proceeded to leave.
Dan gave the Valet the parking ticket for the new Buick he had
driven to the Country Club earlier in the afternoon. When the
car was brought around, the young man who delivered it saw
Dan was not in any shape to drive, and he said so. I thought
Dan was going to take the kid's head off, and the young man
retreated. Then it was my turn… and when Dan got into the
car, I said he should let me drive. He started to yell at the top
of his lungs, saying he was perfectly capable of driving back
to the Pfister Hotel. I knew he was not so I started to plead
with him, but he was belligerent and refused to give me the
keys. Finally, without thinking and completely exasperated,
I hauled off and popped him with a right hook to the end of
his nose. I surprised <u>myself</u> when I did it, and I couldn't have
delivered a luckier shot if I had aimed. Dan's nose exploded
and blood spewed everywhere… on the inside windshield, the
dash board, and all over the baby-blue tuxedo. A moment past

as I cowered in my seat, thinking he was about to retaliate and sorry to have hit him. Suddenly, Dan started to howl… and I thought he was in pain, but I soon realized he was howling with laughter. Perplexed, I waited for an explanation. "Well, I'll be damned!" laughed Dan hardily, "Have you <u>any</u> idea how many guys would <u>love</u> to get in a <u>lucky</u> punch like that?" Of course I had never thought of anything so bizarre. Why <u>would</u> they? But as time went on I learned what he meant, and I witnessed cowardly aggression toward professional football players, and more than once I had to be rescued from a situation because I was in the way of some stranger wanting to show his <u>toughness</u> by taking pot shots at Dan, when Dan wasn't looking. (By the way, he let me drive the car back to the hotel but it took days of soaking to get the blood out of the tuxedo and by the time we finished… it was <u>pale</u>, <u>pale</u> baby-blue.)

Once in Washington, D. C., as I came around a corner, a man sucker-punched Dan, and as he was going down he yelled, "Sandra, get out the front door." I did as I was told and the encounter latest only moments, as Dan soon had the man crying for mercy. He had a head lock on him and he spoke very calmly to the fellow, whispering in his ear the error of his ways. When Dan finally released him, Dan reached out and shook the guy's hand and the man behaved as though Dan was his best friend. It confused me but I concluded it was the only, desperate way, the man felt he could get Dan's attention.

Another time in a bar in Washington, as I came out of the Ladies Room, a punch intended for Dan caught me unexpectedly, and as I hit the floor, a sharp tile made a deep gash in my elbow. It all happened quickly and Dan's friends threw the "hitter" out the front door, and then they rushed to my side to see if I had been badly hurt. I had not, but there was blood everywhere and I should have had it stitched up because it bleed for many hours, but I didn't want to take time out and miss the fun, or spend the money in an Emergency Room. Besides, I was tougher than that!

Dan was proud of me and he introduced me to many well-known persons; Duffy Dougherty, his Michigan State coach; Y.A. Title, the retired N.Y Giants quarterback; and one time, we sat and talked with Dick "Night Train" Lane, the spouse of the late Dinah Washington. It seemed as if he knew almost

everyone and once, he was terribly disappointed I couldn't

accompany him to meet Bear Bryant. I had fallen and sprained

both ankles, but Dan insisted on carrying me into the meeting.

However, I couldn't make it and I didn't go… He told me

I would never have the *opportunity* to meet the <u>Bear</u> again

because Bear Bryant was elderly. Dan didn't want me to miss

the chance, and he had been correct… regrettably, I didn't meet

the Bear… he died shortly thereafter.

The introduction to Y.A. Tittle was at a party in East

Lansing, MI and it is memorable because he and I had a long

discussion about the reason ballplayers pat one another on

the fanny. At the time, there was public conjecture that this

action had sexual overtones… an opinion which both he and I

regarded as <u>utterly</u> ridiculous. In the end we agreed that it is a

<u>loving</u> gesture, much like placing a hand on a baby's derriere to

reassure them; letting them know you are present and they are

loved. (Like I said, "It's all about <u>love</u>.")

One of the most memorable times I had with Dan and some

of the Packers, took place on a week long trip to Miami, Fl where we were invited to the wedding of his friends, Dick Fincher and Jane Lange. Dick was a handsome and wealthy, former Florida State Senator who owned a large automobile dealership, and had at one time been married to the movie actress and entertainer, Gloria De Haven. Dick called Dan, inviting us to the come down for the wedding at his fabulous house on Sunset Island #3, located just off Miami Beach.

The trip down was fun because we ran into the popular, great, Wisconsin full back, Rufus "Roadrunner" Ferguson on the airplane. Rufus was returning to Miami to visit his family. He went on to be inducted into the University of Wisconsin-Football Hall of Fame. (See picture)

We arrived at Dick's home to find Ron Kramer already there. Ron had just undergone surgery on his back, and I found it a wonderment to watch his healing process on a daily basis. At the first of the week Ron could barely walk but, by the end of the week he was almost totally recuperated. No one has ever since been able to convince me that athletes are physically, just-like- everyone-else when it comes to mending their bodies. They are far different and because of their inherent physical energy, strengths, and other qualities, their bodies respond much more quickly to therapy and rest than you and me. His recovery was amazing to watch!

Soon after, Paul Hornung and Max McGee arrived… Tucker Fredrickson, the N.Y Giants running back, was there also, and of course many, many people of the Miami social set. The wedding was a catered affair and the marriage took place by the swimming pool on the back lawn. We all ended up staying until dawn… singing and partying.

The week which followed was just as enjoyable because we were invited to lunches and parties throughout the week. One evening, Max invited us to the Jockey Club where he is a member, and we danced until closing. The next day we went over to his condo, met his daughter who was visiting, and spent the afternoon drinking beer on the patio, and reminiscing about great times in Green Bay. Max was always a sweetheart to me and he made me feel very welcome in his home. (Max took

313

a photo of Dan and me at his condo which I have included.)
(I took many pictures during this fun-filled week which I
didn't want to end, and I have included them also… for your
enjoyment.)

We went to the Packer football games frequently, and going
with Dan was a whole different experience than when I had
gone before with my girlfriends. First of all, we were invited to
bountiful tailgate parties which are held just outside Lambeau
Field. Often we found that we were not dressed in appropriate
gear, given the weather. Dan was used to participating and was
not adept to being a spectator. Once, when we had seats in the
very top row, cold wind and rain poured down and, some kind
fans took pity on us, sharing their rain gear, or we would have
drowned and frozen in Lambeau Field. We hurried to a nearby
watering-hole, drinking Brandy to help us warm up. Friends
and fans soon surrounded us and we had so much fun with
them, it took us an extra day to get home.

Dan had a friend who worked for Kimberly-Clark in the Fox
River Valley, and he and his wife supplied a plenteous feast of

food and drink at the tailgate parties while the wealthy mingled about. Jim Kimberly, one of the heirs to the Kimberly-Clark fortune was there with his wife, Jackie. The Kimberly's liked us and invited us to visit them in Florida. One time when we had flown down for a few days, we called them at there home in West Palm Beach. A maid answered the phone, and then Jackie got on and insisted I come shopping with her on prestigious Worth Avenue. I declined because I didn't have the kind of money necessary to shop in the expensive stores located there. Jackie had been a poor, young showgirl when older Jim had married her, and though I did not state the financial reason for my refusal, she seemed to surmise why I would not come with her, and she kept saying it was okay… "…come anyway and don't worry about it." Later, when the big, sex scandal broke involving Jackie and Roxanne Pulitzer, I learned Jackie had often invited friends to shop with her, and she bought them anything they desired, charging it all to her multi-millionaire husband, Jim. Someone told me Jackie would jet her girlfriends from West Palm to New York City for a day of shopping, and go from the top floor to the bottom floor of the finer stores, and purchase whatever caught the fancy of her and her friends.

Jim Kimberly stuck by her during the trial and troubles, but later they divorced. It is my understanding that in the course of their marriage she spent over $100 million dollars. Jim lost his homes and yachts, and ended up across the river in a little house in Palm Beach, with just enough money to last until he died. "Fortune makes quick dispatch and in a day… can strip you barer than beggary itself." (Kipling) I've wondered what happened to Jackie and I surmise it would be difficult for her to land another wealthy man, with him knowing how she loved to spend money. Of course it's all relative, and if the guy has enough money and the supply is endless, and he loves her enough, maybe she found another. I have often thought about that shopping invitation and what it would have been like, but I am pleased to know I did not contribute to Jim's misfortunes… he was a nice man. (Roxanne Pulitzer wrote a book telling about life in West Palm Beach and the sex scandal in 1989… it is called "The Prize Pulitzer" and she has written other books since.)

As you can tell, Dan Currie and I had a great time together, and I received a pretty good taste of what life is like when one is married or engaged, to a professional football player. It is a life that one can <u>only</u> imagine… fast, exciting and fun. Dan and I did all this on a limited budget… so I can only guess at the times to be had if one is with a very, high-profile, highly-paid, professional athlete.

I was shopping with my little girl in a suburb of Washington D.C. and the wife of one of the Washington Redskins came in to buy a few things. (This was right after the Redskins won Super Bowl XVII in 1991.) She must have shopped there often, because they knew her and fell all over her. I was curious and while standing in the background so I could watch, I saw the staff cater to her every whim. (The staff must have worked on commission) And when she left, she asked for over $10,000. of merchandise to be delivered to her home… and the entire transaction took <u>less</u> than an hour. (*Nice work if you can get it!*)

In 1973 I took a job at a hotel just west of Milwaukee and Dan and I moved to the area, and unbeknown to us our relationship was nose-diving!

(From left to right) Ray and Jackie Nitschke, the author, and Dan
Currie, at the Packer Alumni Weekend Banquet, Green Bay-1972.

We were invited to march in the St. Patrick's Day Parade behind Mayor Daley and the astronaut, Gene Cernan. Our friend, Billy, and date on the right.

Dan and me at a tailgate party outside of Lambeau Field. The little girl is Fuzzy and Susan Ann Thurston's daughter, Victoria, so named because the Packers were victorious many times during the year she was born (1962). Victoria (Tori) now runs her father's company.

(www.FuzzysTicketTours.com or www.Fuzzys63.com)

Dan dries little "Duffy" after a bath.   Photo by author. (1972)

Dan works on his story which was later presented on NFL TODAY.
(1972)

My parents and Dan on a Sunday afternoon picnic in Wisconsin Dells. (Summer-1973)

My parents and me holding our little dog. (Madison, WI -1974)

(From left to right) Me, Rufus "Roadrunner" Ferguson, and Dan on an airplane headed for Miami. (Spring-1973) Rufus is now a member of the University of Wisconsin Football Hall of Fame.

This is the back of Dick Fincher's home, Sunset Island #3, Miami Beach, FL (Spring-1973)

Dan took this picture of me by Fincher's pool about an hour before
the wedding.

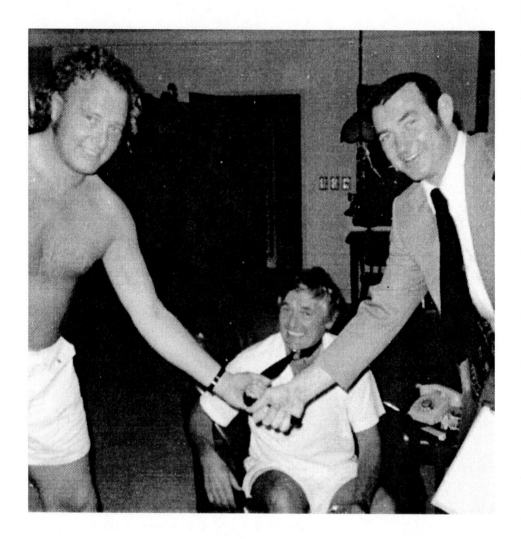

Playfully, Paul Hornung and Dan placed a noose around Dick Fincher's neck, encouraging him to get ready for his wedding.

(From left to right) Max McGee, Paul Hornung (seated), Dick Fincher, unknown, Tucker Fredrickson (New York Giants), Dan Currie, a priest/friend of Fincher's, and a cousin to Dick Fincher. The boys have a few at the bar in Dick's home before the ceremony. The doorway behind Dan goes out to the pool. When this was taken by me, Ron Kramer was out by the pool.

(From left to right) Paul Hornung, Enrique (the Best Man), Dick
Fincher and his bride, Jane Lange. No one could decide exactly
where the right spot would be for the ceremony so we giggled and
walked around the yard for awhile.

Dan and Me by the pool late in the evening after the wedding
reception.

This photo was taken by Max McGee outside his condo in Miami.
(1973)

THE BIG PLAY

My father and mother were disappointed about our relationship. We had not made much progress toward making an honest woman out of me, and living together in the early 1970's was not as socially acceptable as it is today. My parents were saddened because Dan and I had not worked through our difficulties and married. Dan used to make a joke about visiting my parents in our long ranch-style house, saying when the evening was winding down and my father decided it was time for bed, he would summon my mother and me and say, "Okay, girls, time for bed!" We would follow him to the far-end of the house to our respective bedrooms, where windows overlooked a beautiful, lazy river and woodland scene, leaving Dan to sit in the back room <u>alone</u>. Dan quipped to some of our friends, "You have to pay for the room with the view." But in truth, that was <u>exactly</u> my father's point and finally, my father gave Dan a sort of ultimatum…either <u>get</u> married or <u>get</u> going.

Dan decided to <u>get going</u>… he was not going to be told what to do even if he did <u>not</u> think my father was wrong. So… he called an old college teammate, Fran O'Brien, who had a popular bar and restaurant in Washington, D.C., and asked him for a job. Fran O'Brien obliged and in January, 1975 I put Dan on a plane in Milwaukee and watched my dreams fly away with him.

I told myself I was better off without him, but our relationship was far from over and Dan called often, continually reassuring his "Princess" he would make things better for us very soon. I wanted it to be true so I worked hard and kept myself busy. Then in early March a good friend of ours from Appleton by the name of Jake Skall died, and Jake had requested that Dan Currie be one of his pall-bearers. Dan returned to Wisconsin for the funeral and he and I went to it together, after which I took a week-long vacation from work, and accompanied Dan back to Washington, D.C.

A word about Jake Skall...

Jake was a well-known and much-loved restaurant owner in Appleton, WI and many of the Packers frequented his establishment throughout the Lombardi glory years. Fuzzy Thurston loved Jake and vice-versa, and on Jake's 70th Birthday, Fuzzy gave Jake his Super Bowl ring from Super Bowl I to wear until he died. I have put a picture in the book of Fuzzy giving Jake the ring. (*What a guy*! *See what I mean about* <u>*love*</u>!)

The week in Washington was wonderful and it happened to be Saint Patrick's Day, so I got to see how Washingtonians celebrate the big day. I did not want to return from the warm spring weather and the cherry blossoms which were <u>now</u> in bloom, or the excitement of the people and celebrities who stopped in at Fran O'Brien's. When the week was over, I had a hard time leaving Dan and returning to a snowy, winter night, which awaited me in Milwaukee... I was really down.

About a week later, Dan called and said that Fran had made him the night manager in the restaurant, and that would mean more pay. He said he needed "his <u>tomato</u> on his arm" (<u>that</u> would be <u>me</u>) and I should think about moving to Washington. When I told my parents, I thought they were going to die on the spot. This was certainly <u>not</u> what my father had envisioned when he had given Dan the ultimatum. However, I knew if I did not leave Wisconsin on this invitation, I would <u>forever</u> be stuck without ever living somewhere else, and experiencing some of what the rest of the world was like. So in April, I sold our household belongings, kept what I treasured, rented a U-Haul, and all alone journeyed east in search of my destiny.

When I said "Good-bye" to my father he cried, and he told me Washington, D. C. was such a dangerous place for me to go. He begged me to change my mind, but Dad had pulled this on me before, not wanting me to leave home (I am his only child), and even though he succeeded in making me feel guilty, I left. I had to be set free, just once, and I promised I would return home on a monthly basis once I was established, and I did, because at the time one could fly round trip from D.C. to

Madison for about $70. Ironically, my father was correct in his analogy of D.C. and of the dangers which existed there and sure enough, the first weekend I arrived, Human Kindness Day was celebrated on the Mall, and someone was stabbed in the eye. On the other hand, a few days later I was somewhat gratified that there had been a bank robbery in a little town called Hustler, about 10 miles from my Wisconsin home, so Dad couldn't say much, as crime had come to our area, too.

Dan and I found a great apartment in Virginia after we had tried to take over a terrible, hand-me-down place which had belonged to one of the bartenders at Fran O'Brien's. I have never in my life seen such a terrible place. The floor was so sticky from spilled beer and booze that one had to peel their feet from the floor when they walked on it. There were chicken and pork chop bones under the bed. There were no bugs (roaches) now, but there must have once been, because there were at least ten empty cans of Raid on the kitchen counter, and I knew they would soon return. It was definitely not what the "Princess" had envisioned so I was out of there as quickly as my legs would carry me.

Once we got settled in the new place, Dan was offered many invitations from prominent persons in D.C. since he was employed at Fran O'Brien's. When my mother, aunt, and cousin, visited we were given tickets to a concert at the Kennedy Center, sat in the First Lady's box seats, drank champagne and ate dinner, all compliments of Fran's customers. It was a delightful time but in contrast, there were scary times also, and one evening Dan came home shaken. A woman with whom we were somewhat acquainted, was arguing with another woman over a man in the back of Fran's restaurant. As they sat in a booth facing each other, she fired her gun into the wall to scare the other woman. The bullet traveled along the inside concrete wall, hit a steel girder and ricocheted, killing a man who was standing a few feet away from Dan. I didn't tell my father about the incident, because he would have come to get me immediately.

I could tell, and so could Dan, there was friction between Fran O'Brien and his partners. Later, we learned there was a squeeze to take over Fran's interests and to oust him. When it happened, Dan was the first to be fired. It was a terrible blow for us as well as for Fran, and although Dan and I were close and stuck together, I was <u>again</u> carrying the ball as far as finances were concerned. I looked around for employment but I didn't want to commit to a career-type job because I didn't know what was going to happen, so I did temp-work and kept my ears to the ground regarding employment possibilities.

The following months were miserable… we were suffering financially and when finally his car was re-possessed… it was the first and only time in our years together that I saw Dan shed tears. He wasn't feeling sorry for himself, but he was terribly frustrated, and questioned what had gone wrong in his life… what had he done to merit this?… why couldn't things get <u>better</u> instead of <u>always</u> worse? I too, cried… agreeing with him that fate had been unkind… and I cried also, because I did not know what I could do… to make it better. The situation was burdensome for Dan, and he realized my father had been right… and our relationship was straining both of us. I knew it was only a matter of time before something terrible happened to one of us. Though we would not admit it was over between us, we both knew we could not go on… together. I don't think Dan thought I would leave him and I did not want to…but I knew in my heart, I had to move on and start a new life for myself. I knew we were in deep trouble, so I turned to God and prayed for His help. Dan had his own ritual… resting in the living room, partially dozing as he had always done, he read prayer books and inspirational verses to help him make it through the night. Remember… there are saints who sin… and rogues who pray.

In March of 1976, a lady we had known for some time called me and asked if I would fill in for her at her bartending job at a busy Washington restaurant while she had her tonsils removed. I was surprised and told her I had no experience bartending. She said that was great because she didn't want anyone experienced to steal her coveted job while she was absent. I decided to take the two-week job, and for two weeks I found out why she didn't want anyone to get her job… the pay was terrific.

A short time before Dan had been fired from Fran O'Brien's restaurant, Dan and I had lunch at Duke Ziebert's, a restaurant on L Street, and Dan knocked out a front tooth while drinking a bottle of beer. A gentleman sitting at a nearby table motioned for Dan to come over, and introducing himself as having been the dentist for the Redskins, he said he would be happy to fix Dan's tooth the next day if we would come to his office.

The next day Dan and I went to the dental office and the dentist re-cemented the tooth onto Dan's partial plate. Then the dentist asked us out for lunch, and the following Saturday, he invited us to be his guests at Laurel Race Track. We enthusiastically accepted and were shown a great time, as well as winning about $400. on a horse on which the dentist had given us a tip. We liked Doctor Sullivan, and we soon discovered that a lot of other people in Washington D.C. felt the same way about him.

I was <u>diligently</u> saying my prayers, asking God for a sign telling me what I should do… return to Wisconsin… or stay in D.C. I was working at the Club Downunder for the two-week employment, and while I was there the strangest thing started happening. Each time Doctor Sullivan came into the Club my heart fluttered and I became flushed in the face. I couldn't believe it… it was like a memory of a long-ago, high-school crush, and this feeling continued each time I saw him during the two weeks.

By Friday, the last day I was to work, I was totally enamored with Doctor Sullivan, and I decided I had better tell him. It took a lot of guts but I knew how I felt, and I trusted my feelings as a sign from God… this is what he wanted me to do. So I waited until the Doctor came in for lunch, and when the time was right and the restaurant had quieted down, I asked if I could speak with him. He said, "Sure, what do you want?" I said, "Doctor Sullivan, I think I am falling in <u>love</u> with you!" He was flabbergasted and immediately said, "…but, but, I thought you were Danny's girl." I said, "I know you think that and …I am… but our relationship has not been going well for a long time. We have slowly evolved into a friendship, and I guess you could say I have become the sister Dan never had… and… he is the brother that I never had. For the most part… our love affair is over." Doctor Sullivan thought for a moment, and then he said, "Would you care to come out after work tonight, and have a drink with me?" I said, "Yes, I would love it!"

One of the hardest things I ever had to do was to call Dan and tell him how I felt about Doctor Sullivan, and that I was going to have a drink with him later that evening. Dan hesitated a moment, and then, knowingly, he said, "Okay, Princess! Take your best shot!"

Matthew J. Sullivan came to get me at the restaurant on Friday, April 2, 1976 at 9:15 P.M., and for the next 18 years which followed, I rarely left his side.

My future husband, Dr. Matt Sullivan, on a ship in Greece in the early 1960's, during the time I was dating Paul Hornung. Matt, like Paul, went to Notre Dame on a football scholarship.

Matt and me at the Ritz-Carlton, Washington D.C. (Easter- 1978)

Matt and me on our wedding day in front of the Chapel, Fort Myers,
Virginia.

TOUCHDOWN

Risk taking is… to me… what life is all about. You never know the answer unless you ask the question. You never know the result unless you try… and when I approached Dr. Matt Sullivan, and told him I thought I was falling in love with him… I was living at risk. I had made myself vulnerable; he may not have wanted me, and he could have easily told me to "Take a walk!" …but for some reason or other, I said the right words to the right person at the right time. Call it fate, call it luck, or call it the grace of God…but, it was the <u>right</u> move. There was 21 years difference in our ages, but Matt always said that… age is just a number…. and we both agreed with Satchel Page who said, "How old would you be… if you didn't know how old you are?" Of course, we both cared about Dan and we

347

considered it our personal responsibility to make sure that...
Dan Currie was all right.

Many who read this may think I am a heartless person who
goes around hurting people I say I love, and you are right to
a degree. I certainly did hurt someone I love... but I wasn't
heartless. In fact, it broke <u>my</u> heart as well as Dan's when we
separated, and I took special care with the assistance of Dr.
Sullivan, to make sure Dan had everything he needed. We
talked frequently and there was no animosity between us. He
said he wanted to go to Chicago to live, and I physically moved
him there. When the next Christmas rolled around and Dan
wasn't with me, I thought I would die from missing him. Matt
was very understanding about my feelings; knowing that one
does not give up a relationship such as ours, without pain. There
was absolutely no indication of jealousy on the part of Matt or
Dan, and Dan made it known to Matt he wanted me to have the
chance for a better life than he (Dan) could provide. They were
friends and Matt was always concerned for Dan's welfare.

The telling of this part of the story is painful even now... 27

years later, so I will jump ahead and tell you, Dan Currie is fine now. It is also important for me to say that I will <u>always</u> <u>love</u> Dan Currie. Throughout the years he spent many Christmas' with us, usually traveling long distances to be there. When I married Matt, my parents and matron of honor were headed for the elevator in our apartment building, and I made an excuse that I had to go back to the apartment to retrieve something, but in actuality I called Dan. I said, "Danny, I am going now… to marry Matt!" My dear, sweet Dan said, "Go get him, Princess!" When our daughter was 3 months old, Matt and I traveled from D.C. to Las Vegas so Dan could see my little baby. Dan and I have remained good friends throughout all these years, and a month never passes without our talking with each other.

So you see… if I had not taken the job offer in 1961 and worked for the Green Bay Packers, I would not have met and married my husband nor would my daughter, Kerry, have been born. That simple choice directed the course of my life, and one might say <u>here</u> that… God works in strange ways. If you are wondering how my husband handled the knowledge of my wilder days and the fun I had with the Green Bay Packers, it is simple to explain. The day after we were married, he stood in the middle of our living room and said, "I want to get something <u>straight</u>… right from the <u>beginning</u>, Sandy. I know **all** about it… and if you ever <u>stray</u>, even <u>once</u>… it's <u>over</u>!" I got it! I understood the ground rules and I never strayed. In fact after that, it never crossed my mind. (I was a good girl … I was!) I was willing to do whatever it took to make life <u>good</u>, and my life with Matthew Sullivan was good… a fairy tale which had come true. He had a well-established dental practice in Washington, D.C., and his patient roster read like "Who's Who." I was again the "belle of the ball," and my husband, who was proud of me, showed me a lifestyle which I had never <u>before</u> known to exist. Our invitations were from high-raking political persons; U.S. Senators, Congressmen, Generals, Admirals, and foreign dignitaries. We attended functions at many embassies and at unbelievable mansions. We lunched and dined with people who had in some way or other made a name for themselves in Washington. We were members of Congressional Country Club and I spent time golfing with the wives of Washington's elite. We traveled to Ireland and Scotland three times, and while we golfed at St. Andrew's,

Kerry, our little girl, was attended by a nanny and visited the college where the future Prince of Wales, Prince William, would attend. I was treated with the utmost respect because I was **Mrs**. Dr. Sullivan… and in short, I had a wonderful life.

Matt had six grown children from his first married, and I soon grew to love the children as though they were my own. I came into the picture long after he and his first wife had separated, but when they divorced, he took a big financial loss from which he never recovered. Then in 1987, we were caught in the stock market crash, and then suffered further set-backs during the Northeastern recession in the late 80's. We found ourselves in very bad shape financially when Matt sold his dental practice, but did not get paid what had originally been promised. My husband had a life insurance policy from which we borrowed to keep us afloat, and when that was used up, it was my turn, once again, to carry the financial load. Unfortunately, at about the same time, I had to have both of my hips replaced, and suffered from serious back problems, so that cramped my style for awhile. (I was in my early forties when I had the operations.) I did my best for us but there was a lot to be desired, and my husband, now 74, contributed with Social Security and by caring for our daughter and preparing meals, while I pursued a fortune as the Vice-President of a skin-care company out of North Carolina. I never looked back, but kept right on believing… I am a **Champion**. The hours were long and hard and the work was demanding, and I often longed for additional time to spend with my husband and daughter… I love them… so much.

Baby makes three... taken just before we left to have lunch on the White House lawn with President and Mrs. Reagan, as part of the "Superman" movie premier. Christopher Reeves and many other celebrities were present.   Spring-1983

353

Matt, Kerry, and me at a friend's home on the Maryland Eastern
Shore. (Easter-1985)

END ZONE

One afternoon in 1984 my husband, Matthew, told me he was not feeling well and eight days later he was dead! He was buried two days before Christmas in Arlington National Cemetery. The U.S. Navy Band marched in front of a caisson of six white horses, and escorted him to his resting place. I received the folded flag and was offered America's gratitude for his military contribution. As I sat with bowed head, a Naval Officer knelt in front of me and quietly spoke the tribute. My husband was saluted with the firing of twenty-one rounds, and as we left the Cemetery, a bag-piper played "Danny Boy." On Capitol Hill we celebrated Matt's life at a pub where we held an Irish Wake, and background music played over and over... "Cheer, cheer, for old Notre Dame..." He loved Notre Dame,

Sandy Sullivan

his Alma Mater.

The Navy positions to march in front of my husband's caisson.
Note: The Chapel in the background is the same in which we were
married. Fort Myers, Virginia

My husband's caisson.

My husband's Navy honor guard carries him to his resting place

A Naval officer kneels in front of me, gives me the folded American
flag, and speaks a tribute of the nations' appreciation for my
husband's military contribution.

Everyone in the family left the next day and my twelve year old daughter and I, spent Christmas alone. I put up a tree but there were no decorations on it, and I gave my daughter presents but they were not wrapped. To try to lift our spirits we went to Congressional Country Club for dinner on Christmas Night. We were touched by many friends and the Staff at the Club who extended their kindness and condolences to us. It was a very sad evening; it surely wasn't the same without <u>him.</u>

When my husband died, my Mother was in Mayo Clinic recovering from surgery, and my parents could not attend his funeral. I missed them; their absence was sorely felt. My parents loved my husband and they took his death hard. I remember crying on the phone to my Mother, and she, crying also, did her best to soothe me as only a mother can. I said, "No one loves me anymore, Mom." To which she emphatically replied, "Well, **I** love you, Sandy" …a comment which still sticks in my mind and assures me I am loved. Then she said, "Everything will be all right…you just wait and see." And… her words made me feel better.

In April, my parents, both in their late eighties, drove from Wisconsin to Washington, D.C. and brought my daughter and me home. It helped, psychologically and spiritually, to come home. Then I sat down and told my father that we were having financial difficulties and I had very little money left. My father smiled and said, "I understand how you feel, Sandy, your mother and I are broke, too! So, kid, it looks like it's up to you... to support all of us." I couldn't believe my ears! No way!

Dad carried our belongings from the car into the old house where I had grown up. He carefully placed my daughter's things on the bed in my old childhood bedroom, and dumped my things on the floor in the back bedroom, located near the garage. I jokingly said, "Gee, Dad, wasn't this room intended for a <u>maid.</u>" He replied, "Yes, it was, my dear, and <u>you're</u> the maid."

My father may sound harsh to some, and perhaps he was. He was tough on me but he snapped me back... to face reality. The party was over! I knew now...I was either going to sink or swim. Others may think I got what I deserved, but, it doesn't matter what anyone thinks. It didn't matter what I thought either… I still got the job.

There were days I was not very strong and to comfort myself, I dug around in my flower garden, and often found my face covered with mud and tears. It would have been easy to get a gun from the cabinet, and end my life. Believe me, I often wished so many people were not depending on me…then I would have done it for sure. Yeah…right! When something like this happens, one soon finds out whether they want to live, or not… what they are really made of… it's a big decision. One either takes the easy way… and ends it… or the tough way… finds the courage, and starts all over, again… I chose the latter. I also learned about the <u>kiss of death</u>…the <u>greatest</u> danger… <u>feeling sorry for myself</u>. The minute I did … I was as good as dead.

I was in a state of metamorphosis… like a caterpillar dying in order to become a butterfly. I was being pruned… cut to the quick, and it hurt. Just as we cut back rose bushes, enabling them to bloom and flourish again, this was my time of painful, quiet waiting; a time of dormancy. It was an opportunity for me to silently heal and quietly grow… and I would bloom again… I knew it. Though it was to be… a long and inactive season, I tried to be patient. My husband often referred to me as his "filly," and I promised myself this <u>winning filly</u> would race again. I could smell the roses, and I imagined a blanket of them cloaking my shoulders while advancing to the <u>winner's circle</u>. Victory would be mine… someday… but I am so impatient. (*Sandra, please, <u>patience</u>! Endure it… wait your turn.*)

I tried to find a way to make a living and thank goodness, I had gone to college. Jerry Kramer's insistence of me getting a college degree was a life-saver. I worked hard; did some teaching and tried to take care of everyone. There was too much work, too little time, and even less money. My wonderful mother died the next year, and I knew if I mourned her the same way I had grieved over my husband, I <u>definitely</u> would not survive. My health took a big hit! It showed and I went into a deep depression, and had a hard time pulling out of it… I was <u>not</u> well. Mentally, I survived by praying much of the time. I didn't ask God for anything, but thanked Him for having given me so much of everything… bad times and good! I placed my complete <u>trust</u> in Him.

My daughter is extremely important to me and I needed to sustain my strength for her. I had promised my husband I would be there and get her through college… it was difficult; raising her, supporting us, and caring for my aging father. Two of my husband's children (my stepchildren) were very kind to us. They could not support us financially, although on occasion they helped, but they always gave us their time, love, and encouragement. (My thanks to Colleen and Ray, and Chris and Mimi; how you have <u>blessed</u> us!)

My father continued to live in my care for eight more years. They were hard years, but they are some of the best years of my life. One of my greatest accomplishments is in knowing I did my best to make him happy and comfortable, and in doing so, I atoned for a lot of sins. Dad and I were very close… I didn't love the <u>work</u> which his care required, but I loved doing the work <u>for him</u>. One of the last things I said to him is, "I <u>know</u> I gave you some anxious moments, Pa. I'm sorry for that… but I am going to be <u>okay</u>! <u>You</u> know that, don't you? I love you, Dad!" He nodded and said, "I love you, too, <u>Sandy</u>." My name was the last word he spoke… he didn't say anything after that… I was with him when he died…my pa.

MONDAY MORNING QUARTERBACK

If I could do it again… would I do it differently? I doubt it. Would I still be crazy about football players? Probably! Green Bay Packers? Yes, of course! I <u>love</u> them… they are in my blood. This is a <u>love</u> story and this is what the love story is about… **<u>LIVING!</u>** Knowing my Packer friends is like threading them through a needle in my youth, and weaving them into the fabric of my life. I have securely stitched them into the lining of my heart, so I can not possibly lose the feeling, or forget what it was like to be around them…to be young, full of passion, and on **<u>fire</u>**… to never forget how thrilling it is… just to be <u>alive</u>! They've always made me feel so alive and they showed me… that I too, am a **winner**. What I did in my youth, I did because it is the only way I could become me and… I'm not sorry… I had a lot of fun… <u>few regrets</u>! Besides, I am a Senior citizen now, and even though my youth was wild, I must say, having all those wild times helped me become a really <u>solid</u> citizen. I must have had a good time because I am still talking about it 40 years later. I only look back to smile!

Some mistakenly thought I would marry soon after my husband's death. Why would I? I was 39 years old before I married my husband. I had certainly taken my time, shopped around, kissed enough toads, and found Prince Charming. I am in no hurry to try and find another. This time he will have to find me.

Others think I should marry for money. Could I sleep my way to the top? Maybe! But I am <u>not</u> going to! And trust me, baby, when you have <u>no</u> money, the affluent men don't want you… when you are down and out, they are <u>nowhere to be found</u>. In my opinion, the worst time to marry is when you are broke. Marrying a guy for money enslaves <u>you</u> to his whims. For me, marriage for money would be like selling myself into bondage. I have taken care of <u>too many</u> people to "submit my neck into another yoke"…and for a few bucks. Forget it! I'll make it on my own. I have the *opportunity* and I am going to do just that. Once I am rich again… and I will be… maybe then I will think about re-marrying. I'll see! One thing is for sure… the "chaps" who wouldn't help me in the past few years haven't a prayer if they show up after the bonanza.

Mostly, I want my life's experiences; the struggle and the survival… to serve as an example to my daughter, granddaughters, and great-granddaughters, and to anyone else who needs an example. I want them to **live…** I want them to **dance**. Perhaps one day they, too, may find themselves in an uncomfortable situation without means… and they can look at my life and say… "Hey, if **she** made it…**so can I**!"

Regarding relationships…

I have not had a relationship because I have been too busy surviving and staying alive. A relationship, if you are going to do it **right**, takes time and a lot of energy. Besides, exceeding the experiences of my life could be a tough act to follow, and not many fellows are up for a game of "Can you **top** this?"

Maybe, someday! Who knows? It could happen that one day a fine person comes into my life, and I will fall deeply in love, <u>again</u>. *Ha*! Did you get a little chuckle out of that? Did you? Well, go ahead and laugh… but, I'm one who believes it is <u>never</u> too late for <u>anything</u>. I believe it! Divine Providence has delivered the goods up to now, and I am anticipating a <u>grand finale</u>. It'll happen…and when it does, I'll know it… and I'm going for it… the brass ring, the gold ring, and all! As for right now, I'm <u>ending</u> this love story. Got to go! Some old friends are waiting for me in Green Bay.

THE LESSON

It's very simple!

<u>Give Life your greatest effort and do everything with love!</u>

WHY?

(*because... <u>unlike football, Life has no replay</u>!*)

Taken from the top of the stairs-Packer Locker Room. The doors
at the bottom... open out to a tunnel and then onto Lambeau Field.
(Circa 1965) From the collection of Vernon Biever (copyright)

The Reward

References:

Bradshaw, T.; (2002) Keep It Simple, (2002) New York: Altria Books. p. v

Carroll, B., Gershman, M., Neft, D., Silverman, M., Thorn, J., (1998) (Elias Sports Bureau); NFL Total Packers, *The Official Encyclopedia of the Green Bay Packers,* New York: Harper Perennial. (brief facts and dates as allowed)

Johnson, C., (1961) The Green Bay Packers, *Pro Football's Pioneer Team,* New York: Thomas Nelson & Sons.

Lombardi, V.T., (1973) Vince Lombardi on Football, New York: Graphic Society Ltd., Connecticut: Wallynn, Inc., volume II, p. 164

Photo credits:

My special thanks go to Vernon J. Biever for his assistance in finding photos from his collection which work with my text. Vern, you're the best!

I want to acknowledge the work of Loughhead Photography, Dallas, TX (copyright) for the 1962 official and unofficial team photo. Unofficial photo is stamped by Loughhead (on the back) and was found in the personal collection of Dan Currie, and used with his permission. Every effort has been made to locate this photographic source. Contact has been made through the Dallas Cowboys Marketing office for whereabouts of Jimmy Bradford, the son-in-law of Loughhead, who I am told, handles the late photographer's work, but who has not responded to inquiries and/or messages. If you read this, please come forward.

Thanks to Ron Kramer for the picture of Vince Lombardi and Ron Kramer, from the personal collection of Ron Kramer, printed with his permission. This picture appeared in the Detroit Free Press but we can not find the name of the photographer or the date it was taken. The person who took this picture is encouraged to come forth with proof and receive credit for the picture.

Photographers of any pictures in this book, for which you have not been given credit, please come forward. I have made every effort to contact you and give you the credit you deserve. Thank you.

Thanks for reading this book. Make <u>your</u> life a <u>love story</u>!

About the Author

Sandy Sullivan is a college instructor, motivational/public speaker, and author. She works passionately to keep the memories of the Glory Days alive in the minds of football fans everywhere. She advocates living life with the same commitment that the men of Lombardi played football; with <u>love</u>. Her company promotes personal appearances of the Green Bay Champions. She currently resides in Wisconsin with her family.

Jacket designed by Jim Mayfield.
Front cover photos from the collection of Vernon Biever ©
Collage by Kerry Sullivan
Printed in U.S.A.

Printed in the United States
21218LVS00004B/8